Fall Wildflowers

of the Blue Ridge

and Great Smoky Mountains

Fall Wildflowers
of the Blue Ridge
and Great Smoky Mountains

Oscar W. Gupton and Fred C. Swope
Department of Biology
Virginia Military Institute

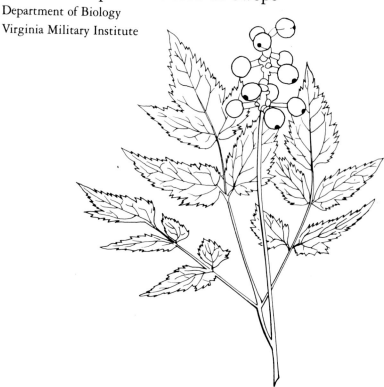

University Press of Virginia

Charlottesville

13235906

(R)

THE UNIVERSITY PRESS OF VIRGINIA
Copyright © 1987 by the Rector and Visitors
of the University of Virginia

Second printing 1989

Library of Congress Cataloging-in-Publication Data

Gupton, Oscar W.
  Fall wildflowers of the Blue Ridge and Great Smoky
Mountains.

  Bibliography: p.
  Includes index.
   1. Wild flowers—Blue Ridge Mountains—Identification.
  2. Wild flowers—Great Smoky Mountains (N.C. and Tenn.)
—Identification.   I. Swope, Fred C.   II. Title.
QK122.3.G87   1987   582.13'09755   86-15666
ISBN 0-8139-1123-0

Printed in Singapore

For

Rosie, Sal, Mayme, Ruby,
and Ruth

Contents

Introduction

Love of nature prompts many of us to lay aside burdensome indoor pursuits and steal away to some favorite refuge. There are many of these shelters from tedium and tension available to us in our wild treasury. Woodlands, thickets, fields, and streams abound in the various geographic provinces, each with its own special charm. Some find their escape in the level lands and shifting dunes of the coastal plain, while others choose the rolling contours of the foothills. There are still others though who find it difficult or impossible to resist the allure of the peaks and gorges of the mountains, and in this part of the country two choice ranges are the Blue Ridge and Great Smokies.

On the crests and in the coves and ravines of these mountains there are endless processions of aesthetically appealing changes of form and color through the seasons. But of all the attractions displayed by the workings of nature, wildflowers are by a long measure the most magnetic. The warming of the air and the greening of the land that come when winter lets go and spring takes hold also bring the floral colors that are so welcome after the cold and somber months of hibernation. The urge to get outside and explore is intensified, and this time of the year is the high point of activities involved with wildflower pilgrimages.

The multicolored landscape of spring is vivid, and the response to it is strong and positive, yet autumn too has many artistic offerings that too often go unnoticed. The pied foliage of the fall of the year is a popular item, but much of the observation here is done from an automobile. So many of the interestingly structured and beautifully colored fruits of wildflowers are not of great size, and a little time taken for a closer look is required in order to gain any real appreciation of their intricacies.

The plants included here are members of the flora of the

Blue Ridge and Great Smoky Mountains. Most are native to the area, and some are introductions that have become established here. Many of these can be seen along roadsides, in open fields, and at the borders of wooded areas, while others require a walk away from the road to visit habitats that have been left more or less undisturbed. Most of the species are fairly common to these mountains with a very few included that are not very plentiful anywhere.

It is hoped that some acquaintance with the beauty of the fruiting condition of these plants might heighten interest in the autumn season, and that this coupled with the more widespread knowledge of the attractiveness of flowers, would contribute to the efforts of all those who, because of their interest in and concern for the preservation of wild things, seek to make us more aware of the value of their presence.

This book is designed to aid in the identification of some of the wildflowers by those without previous training in plant biology. Color photographs taken in the field under natural light conditions are arranged according to fruit color and fruiting period. The descriptions of each plant are written in nontechnical language requiring neither background information about plant structure nor the use of a glossary or diagram.

This volume comprises photographs of 100 species that include some trees, shrubs, vines, and herbs. There are 93 genera and 50 families represented by the photographed species, and there are 124 citations of additional species that give distinguishing characteristics for identification. This provides a guide to 224 species. Many of these plants are found in comparable territory outside this area, so that the usefulness of the information is not restricted to the immediate vicinity.

OSCAR W. GUPTON
FRED C. SWOPE

Lexington, Virginia

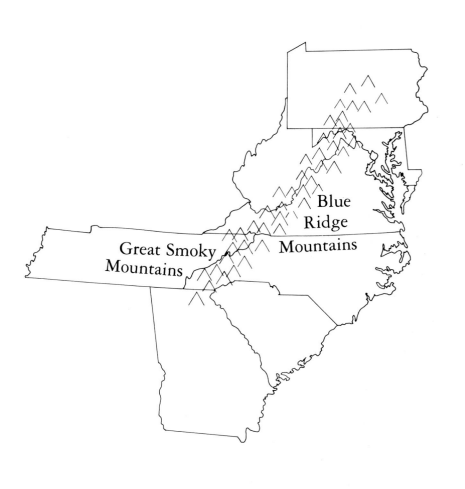

Blue
Ridge
Mountains

Great Smoky
Mountains

Format

The plants are arranged in four groups according to fruit colors. These are variable with gradations accompanying the advancing stages of maturation. In view of this, the groups used herein are composites of hues that often occur and are sometimes blended as fruit ripening progresses. The groups are placed in the following order: green-white-yellow; red-pink-orange; brown-black; blue-purple. They are paged respectively with tabs of green, red, brown, and blue.

Within each of the fruit color groups the plants are arranged in order of the time of fruiting.

The information pertaining to each species is given in the same order throughout:

Common name of species	Common name of family
Scientific name of species	Scientific name of family

Description:

General appearance is indicated by comments on the size, most noticeable features, and environmental association.

Stem character is stated with respect to the size, color, texture, and pattern of branching.

Leaf character is pointed out by noting shape, size, arrangement, and color.

Floral character is delineated by giving shape, size, color, arrangement, number, and time of flowering.

Fruit character is cited in relation to shape, size, color and color changes, edibility, and time of fruiting.

Other species similar to the one depicted are cited along with their distinguishing characteristics.

Medicinal or culinary value of the various parts of the plant are noted.

Poisonous nature of the species is remarked when it is known that its toxicity has resulted in illness.

Miscellaneous items of general interest may be included.

Other names that have been given to the species are entered.

Habitat or type of environment in which the plant grows naturally is cited.

Suitability for planting in wildflower gardens or as an ornamental is indicated.

Propagation methods are given for those species considered suitable for planting.

The scientific names follow the eighth edition of *Gray's Manual of Botany,* and a guide to pronunciation is included.

The works listed below are plant manuals with keys consisting of technical information for identification of the plants of the eastern United States.

Fernald, M. L. 1950. *Gray's Manual of Botany.* Eighth edition, American Book Company.

Gleason, M. A. 1952. *Illustrated Flora of the Northeastern United States and Adjacent Canada.* The New York Botanical Garden.

Gleason, M. A. and A. Cronquist. 1963. *Manual of the Vascular Plants of Northeastern United States and Adjacent Canada.* D. Van Nostrand Company.

Radford, A. E., H. E. Ahles, and C. R. Bell. 1968. *Manual of the Vascular Flora of the Carolinas.* University of North Carolina Press, Chapel Hill.

Rickett, N. W. 1953. *Wildflowers of the United States.* Crown Publishers.

Fall Wildflowers

of the Blue Ridge

and Great Smoky Mountains

A height of 1 foot to about 3 feet is common for the plant. From the base of the stem arise long-stalked leaves with the blades divided progressively into three segments. This pattern of division and subdivision into smaller segments is continued throughout the plant, and the upper leaves become gradually smaller and stalkless. The deep green of the upper surfaces of the numerous small leaflets contrasted with their pale, bluish white undersides provides a handsome foliage.

Wild Columbine is probably as well known and as much a favorite as any of the wildflowers, and the part of the plant primarily responsible for this is, of course, the brightly bicolored and uniquely structured flower, After the scarlet and yellow of the 5-spurred nodding flower has faded and fallen, there is assembled from the remaining floral parts a fruiting arrangement of interesting design.

Each flower forms 5 slender, curved, and pointed pods, each resembling a miniature banana at the tip of which projects a long style that exceeds the length of the pod. These 5 fruits develop side by side at their bases but diverge upwardly to form a starlike pattern, and maturation brings a turning of the supporting stalk from the nodding position of the flower to a skyward orientation of the fruits.

A European species, *A. vulgaris,* with blue, white, pink, or purple flowers escapes cultivation farther north but has not established itself here.

Wild Columbine has also acquired the names Honeysuckle, Meetinghouses, and Rock Bells.

It is found on rocky, wooded, or open slopes, rocky ledges of cliffs, pastures, and roadsides. Propagation of this perennial herb is by seed sown in well-drained soil. All members of the genus appear to hybridize freely.

Wild Columbine

Crowfoot Family

Aquilegia canadensis

Ranunculaceae

On chancing upon this species, one might think he is observing a number of green butterflies hovering near the ground. This image is projected by the cluster of long-stalked leaves that have their blades deeply divided into twin segments.

In April and May the leafless flower stalks stand taller than the incompletely developed leaves and bear a single terminal flower that is about 1 inch in diameter and has 8 white petals.

When the expanding leaves attain their maximum size in June, they exceed the height of the old flowering stems, which now bear the mature fruits. The fruits are pods about an inch long and pear-shaped, with the upper end larger. The pod ranges in color from green to yellowish green or yellow capped with a darker green lid having a central pointed tip.

Use of the roots of Twinleaf as the source of ingredients for a tonic has given it the name Rheumatism Root.

The genus of which this plant and one other species in Manchuria are members was named in commemoration of Thomas Jefferson.

Twinleaf is a perennial herb that grows in rich woods and seems to do especially well in soils of high calcium content. It can be propagated by seeds sown in summer or held at winter temperatures and planted in very early spring. The flowers are short-lived, but the foliage and fruits are interesting and attractive additions to wildflower gardens.

Twinleaf

Jeffersonia diphylla

The branching, smooth green stems grow to a height of 1 or 2 feet. There are rounded oblong leaves near the base of the plant that soon drop off, leaving only the upper stem foliage, which resembles an array of light green arrowheads. These upper leaves have no stalks and taper gradually to a long, pointed tip, while at the basal end a pointed lobe protrudes on either side of the stem.

The flowers of May and June are white and very small; consequently their color contribution is not very noticeable, but the fruits that develop from these flowers do add a series of intriguing structures that are trademarks of the species.

The seeds develop on either side of a papery membrane enclosed within a markedly flattened pod that is oval to circular, with a deep, narrow notch at the upper end. Several to many of these disklike fruits in various stages of maturity are displayed in an elongated cluster.

There is another species, *T. perfoliatum,* that is very similar, but the fruits are about half as large with a shallower, wider notch that gives a heart-shaped appearance.

Both of these plants were introduced from Europe and have established themselves on roadsides, in fields, and in cultivated ground.

Field Penny Cress has also been named Fanweed and Frenchweed.

Some of the larger plants have attractive form and are occasionally planted in wildflower gardens. They are propagated easily from seed and grow in almost any kind of soil in an open area.

Field Penny Cress

Mustard Family

Thlaspi arvense

Cruciferae

The eye-catching feature of this graceful plant is a bright red solitary flower at the end of a straight, slender stalk. This is set off by the curves of stalks bearing nodding buds and by the many-lobed, and often finely cut, leaves.

The stems are 1 foot to 2 feet tall, usually with few or no branches, and both stems and leaves are covered with stiff hairs.

Flowers are present from May to June, and although their showiness attracts the most attention to the plant, they have a very short life. Petals may drop from the slightest disturbance sometimes within a day after the opening of the bud.

The fruit that develops in June and July has the form of an oblong pod tapered to the base. The smooth surface is green with pale vertical streaks, and the apex is a light tan sculptured disk with tiny ridges extending from the scalloped edge to a peak in the center. The seeds are released from pores just beneath the edge of the disk.

Opium is collected from another species, *P. somniferum*, by cutting the immature fruits for the milky juice; morphine and codeine are isolated from this source. Poppy seeds do not contain narcotic properties.

Some other species of this genus are in cultivation but rarely escape to the wild, and all of them are introduced from Europe.

The habitat is almost always disturbed land such as roadsides, fields, railroads, and cultivated fields. Propagation can be effected by seeds sown in late summer.

Poppy
Papaver dubium

The general appearance is that of a yellow-flowered shamrock with a sprinkling of diminutive candelabra. The plant is covered throughout with soft, white hairs, and from the branching stems are extended the long-stalked leaves with their bright green heart-shaped segments. During the long flowering period, the showy blossoms are produced in small clusters and then replaced by the angular picklelike fruits supported on ascending stalks.

This plant grows as much as 1 or 2 feet in height, frequently taking on a leaning posture. The stem usually branches several times near the base and bears a dense cluster of the cloverlike leaves.

Flowering begins in April and continues until October, producing bright yellow flowers about one-half inch across and arranged in small clusters of generally 2 to 8.

Fruiting peaks in June and July, and the slender pointed pods on their ascending stalks are suggestive of candlesticks.

Wood sorrels are generally similar, but *O. montana* and *O. violacea* appear stemless; the former has solitary white or pink flowers, while the latter has clusters of 2 or more purple or white flowers. *O. grandis* is larger in all parts with purplish leaf borders. *O. stricta* and *O. florida* have downswept fruit stalks, and the latter has hairless fruits.

Lady's Sorrel is also called Yellow Wood Sorrel, Yellow Sheep Sorrel, and Sour Grass. This last name pertains to the taste caused by oxalic acid contained in all species, which has caused the plants to be used as a source of flavoring for soups and salads.

This herbaceous perennial grows in open woods, fields, roadsides, and lawns. It may be grown from seeds or the underground parts and is an attractive species; however, the flowers and leaves do often close during cloudy weather.

Lady's Sorrel

Oxalis europaea

Wood Sorrel Family
Oxalidaceae

In late spring and summer large, bright yellow flower heads appear in open fields and along roadsides. They grace the tips of stout, leafy stems that grow to a height of 1 foot to 3 feet. The flowering arrangement is handsome both in form and color, but the fruiting transformation that follows brings on a beauty of a different kind that is more striking than that of the blossoms. Dense, long-stalked tufts of silvery plumes collectively fashion great fluffy and glistening spheres that sit like pom-poms atop the ends of the stems.

From the large taproots arise shoots that in general appearance are in some measure remindful of miniature stalks of corn. The thick, straight stems bear large, clasping, and grasslike leaves with long and pointed blades.

The yellow flowers that open from May to July are small, but they are arranged in tightly packed clusters about 2 inches broad that are sometimes mistaken for a single large flower. Slenderly pointed spikelike bracts radiate from just beneath the flower cluster and extend beyond the flowers, and the stem just at the base of the flower head is swollen.

The cylindrical fruits are about a half-inch long with a slender bristle that is topped with a tuft of feathery branches.

Goat's Beard is an introduction from Europe that has become established in this flora along with two other similar species, *T. pratensis* and *T. porrifolius*. The stem of the former is not enlarged beneath the flower, and the latter has purple flowers. This purple-flowered plant is Salsify, the vegetable cultivated for its edible taproot that has a flavor likened to oysters. This has resulted in the names Vegetable Oyster and Oyster Plant.

All three of these plants grow very well in open habitats with full sun exposure. They are all attractive in flower and in fruit and can be propagated from seeds sown in the early spring.

Goat's Beard

Tragopogon major

Composite Family

Compositae

The rounded crown of this handsome tree rises to a height of 70 to 80 feet. Many of the lower limbs slant earthward, and the dark, reddish brown, scaling, aromatic bark resembles that of cherry. The smooth, glossy stems are copper colored and have the pungent flavor of wintergreen. From the slenderly pointed and lustrous leaves arises a spicy fragrance. The minute male flowers hang in pendulous yellow and stringlike clusters in the springtime, while in the fall the tiny fruits are formed in oval, conelike structures that jut from the stems and undergo a transition from green to yellow to brown.

The leaves are about 2 to 4 inches long with notched bases and finely toothed margins.

The minute flowers come in April and May. The males are in 2- to 4-inch clusters, while the females develop into fruits in "cones" about an inch and a half long during July and August. These "cones" are not as often seen, and the small, winged and disklike fruits are likely to go altogether unnoticed.

The yellowish bark of *B. lutea* identifies it. The white to grayish bark separates the rare *B. papyrifera* and rarer *B. populifolia*; the former has scaling bark. *B. nigra*, common, has very dark scaling bark and wedge-shaped leaf bases. *B. uber*, only recently rediscovered in Smyth County, Virginia, has nearly round leaves.

The stems of Cherry Birch, also called Sweet Birch, Black Birch, and Mountain Mahogany, are cited as "chewing sticks" for the cleaning of teeth.

It is a tree of rich moist woods, steep dry slopes, and shrubby areas which is ornamental in form and fruit, and colorful in its golden autumn foliage. It can be propagated by seeds sown in the fall. Seeds should be thickly sown, since the percentage of germination is low.

Cherry Birch

Betula lenta

During the summer and autumn on the shaded slopes and ravines of moist woods, in the wet soils of marshes, and along stream banks, rather thick colonies of Orange Touch-me-not are common sights. The orange hues of the flowers make them highly visible as well as attractive, and their curious shapes make identification an easy matter. The fruits develop and mature in the late summer and autumn, and it is the manner of their ripening that has given the plant its name. The fruits respond to the slightest touch by snapping explosively apart into five pieces and forcibly scattering the seeds.

The plant is usually 2 to 5 feet tall, and the smooth, slender stems branch freely to produce an irregularly rounded pattern of growth.

The soft, thin leaves are about 5 inches long. They are oval and pointed with toothed margins and pale green or whitish undersides.

Flowers bloom from June to August and may vary from pale yellowish orange to deep orange-red. The closed end of the flower projects as a hooked spur.

Fruiting in August and September produces pressure-sensitive pods not quite an inch long with light and dark green stripes.

There is another species, *I. pallida,* that is very similar in form and grows in the same places, but its flowers are bright yellow.

Orange Touch-me-not also has been given the names Spotted Touch-me-not or Snapweed, Jewelweed, and Celandine.

The crushed leaves and stems used as a swab are reported to prevent or in some measure reduce the toxic effects of poison ivy. Another interesting thing about the leaves is their resemblance to metal foil when held under water in bright sunlight.

This plant can be found in almost any shady and moist places. It can be grown from seeds and is an attractive annual herb with interesting features.

Orange Touch-me-not

Touch-me-not Family

Impatiens capensis

Balsaminaceae

A highly ornamental tree in foliage, flower, and fruit, it is commonly 30 to 60 feet tall, but it may be in excess of 100 feet. Its form is somewhat irregularly pyramidal, and it is generally taller than broad.

The foliage is abundant and handsome in color and form. The large, light green leaves are broadly ovate to heart-shaped, and their smooth, unlobed margins taper gradually to a slender point. They grow in pairs or in circles of 3, and many of them measure a foot in length and more than half a foot in width.

A conspicuous and yet elegant display of color is seen when the shift into floral phase occurs in May and June. A liberal sprinkling of flower clusters appears over the crown of this tree from top to bottom. The large white flowers are yellow-striped and purple-spotted within and are 2 inches wide.

The long, slender fruits appear in June and mature during July and August. They remain hanging in bunches on the tree throughout the winter. These green to brown "cigars" are elongated pointed pods about one-half-inch thick and frequently more than one and a half feet long.

There is another similar species, *C. bignonioides,* that has smaller flowers with more purple within and leaves that have more abruptly tapered points and an unpleasant odor when bruised.

Cigar Tree is also known by its generic name, Catalpa, and as Hardy Catalpa, Western Catalpa, Northern Catalpa, Catawba Tree, Indian Cigar Tree, and Indian Bean.

This is a species native to Tennessee and several other states to the west that has been cultivated as an ornamental and escaped into moist woods.

It is certainly a desirable plant where it can be accommodated. Propagation is by seed sown in the spring or by cuttings.

Cigar Tree

Catalpa speciosa

Bignonia Family

Bignoniaceae

The many colors of flowers, foliage greenery of varying hues, the forms and changing pigmentations of ripening fruits, and the reds and golds that precede the dropping of leaves in autumn are the things that usually attract our attention to the vegetation around us. Sometimes the interaction of the plants with other forms of life will provide yet other points of interest. Such a one that is often quite unusual and quite conspicuous is the plant gall.

Plant galls may be caused by viruses, bacteria, fungi, and several kinds of animals, notably insects. The cells of the host plant are stimulated to grow rapidly and produce enlargements of various shapes and colors in accordance with the particular species of infesting parasite.

The structures seen here on Heartleaf Willow are sometimes mistaken for the products usually seen on plants, such as buds or fruits. Instead they are the results of a parasite-host relationship. Heartleaf Willow and other species of willow produce the Pine Cone Gall in response to infestation by the gall gnat, *Rhabdophaga strobiloides.* The insect eggs are deposited by the female gall gnat in the young buds in the early spring, and the larvae develop through the summer and winter within the gall that results from the invasion.

At the insect's point of entry, the cells of the willow accelerate in growth and produce many layers of tissues. These develop as a series of overlapping scales that take the shape of a cone about an inch and a half long and an inch in diameter. These white to silvery gray galls are conspicuous at the ends of the willow stems and do indeed resemble small pine cones. There are often large numbers of these galls on a host plant.

A common denominator of plant and animal tumors is the production of an enlargement as a result of very rapid and uncontrolled growth rate.

Heartleaf Willow grows along stream banks, by ponds, and in wet thickets.

Heartleaf Willow

Salix rigida

Willow Family

Salicaceae

Because it inhabits areas of disturbed soils, this species is a familiar element of fields and roadsides and thus is one of the most common and commonly seen of the milkweeds. The flowers are not among the brightest or most colorful of the genus, but the fruiting structures are distinctive in their spiny appearance. Moreover, the silvery clouds that envelop the plant and escape upon the breeze into the air when seeds are released serve to earmark the autumn season. Finally, the split and empty pods are left hanging on the dead stems far into the winter, reminders of the time past.

The rough, unbranched stems of this plant are thick and tall, frequently reaching a height in excess of 10 feet.

The broad leaves, sometimes a foot long, grow in pairs and are thickly hairy beneath. Their veining pattern is conspicuous and attractive with the midrib usually tinted pink-purple.

Large rounded clusers of dull pinkish to greenish purple flowers are present among the upper leaves from June to August.

The fruits are gray, curved, and pointed pods about 4 to 5 inches long studded with rows of soft spines. The numerous flat brown seeds are tufted with an abundance of long, soft, and silvery hairs.

The species A. *amplexicaulis* and A. *incarnata* are somewhat similar, but both have smooth fruits; the former has flowers only at the stem tip and stalkless leaves, while the latter has narrower leaves and pink flowers.

Young stems and leaves of Common Milkweed, also called Silkweed, have been cooked and eaten; however, the plant is cited as a poisonous one.

The many roadsides, fields, thickets, and meadows populated by colonies of this species are often enhanced in appearance by the foliage effect. The plant can be propagated by seeds or by segments of the underground stems.

Common Milkweed

Asclepias syriaca

Milkweed Family
Asclepiadaceae

Virgin's Bower, true to its name, does indeed form a thickly tangled mass of intertwined stems fashioning a cushion that sprawls on the ground or climbs upon other plants or on fences. As summer is ending, this bower symbolically proclaims its purity as masses of flowers change the color to white. When the blooming has run its course, the message is reiterated by a second cloak of whiteness as great quantities of densely clustered fruits in their progress through the ritual acts of maturation acquire long, gracefully curving and feathery tails with a silvery sheen.

The leaves of this herbaceous vine are arranged in pairs along the stem, each one consisting of 3 ovate leaflets with large teeth and sometimes lobes. The plant climbs by means of the leaf stalks twining around a supporting structure.

The flowers form a white cross about an inch wide with a central cluster of yellow stamens. They develop from July to September in large, long-stalked clusters.

The vines are cloudy with the flood of fruits that come in September and October. Numerous tiny brown to reddish brown seedlike fruits develop from a single flower, each with a silvered curling plume about an inch long.

There is another species, *C. dioscoreifolia,* that is similar to Virgin's Bower. It is not as common a vine and has its leaves usually divided into 5 leaflets that may have wavy or lobed margins but no teeth.

Virgin's Bower has also been called Devil's Darning Needle. It finds a home in low woods and thickets and along stream banks and fencerows.

It is sometimes cultivated and trained onto fences, trellises, and porches. A hardy species with attractive foliage, a very showy display of flowers, and interesting fruits, it does best in rich soil and is easily grown from seed.

Virgin's Bower

Clematis virginiana

Crowfoot Family

Ranunculaceae

At the peak of its flowering period, this plant is difficult to match in sheer elegance. The large size, the soft colors, and the abundance of the flowers mingled with the dark green and lustrous foliage create a strikingly harmonious blending of superior qualities.

The occurrence of this species on the high ground of peaks and ridges and along the open areas of wood borders and along road embankments makes it highly visible and thus a longtime favorite of wildflower enthusiasts at the height of its spring floral display. Late summer and fall, however, bring other, less well known features with their own shapes and colors. The fuzzy fruits are greenish bronze to reddish brown and develop in a cluster that is reminiscent of a miniature colony of cattails.

This evergreen shrub, or small tree, is commonly 8 to 10 feet tall but may be taller. The leathery leaves are shiny above, whitish beneath, and 3 to 6 inches long. They are smooth on the margins and rounded at both ends.

The large flowers are lilac to purple with greenish spotting within and are 2 inches or more across. They open in large, dense clusters during May and June. From August to October the fruits are formed as oblong capsules covered by a dense growth of rust-colored hairs.

A larger shrub, or small tree, *R. maximum,* has white to pink flowers with yellowish orange spots within and longer leaves that are narrowed or pointed at both ends.

Purple Rhododendron, also called Mountain Rosebay, Rosebay, Purple Laurel, and Catawba Rhododendron, inhabits high and relatively open areas of mountain woods. It and other rhododendrons are widely cultivated as ornamentals and are handled by practically all nurseries.

Purple Rhododendron

Rhododendron catawbiense

Heath Family

Ericaceae

The arid banks of hot and dusty roadsides and the fence-rows adjacent to them many times support a vine that trails and climbs over them, producing in summer flowers that suggest a horticultural cultivar bred for its exotic colors and intricacy of design. Indeed this species is a member of a storied group of plants that have drawn forth some interesting reactions from the humans that chanced upon them. Both the scientific and the common names arose from the belief that the extraordinary structure of the flower represented constituents of the Crucifixion. There were some who interpreted it as a command to spread the Christian faith, and it is said that there were those who, experiencing so great a feeling of awe, were fearful of revealing that they had seen such a flower.

The stems trail along the ground or climb by means of slender twining tendrils. The foliage consists of leaves with blades deeply cleft into 3 or 5 lobes that are pointed and have fine teeth on the margins.

The unique flowers measure about an inch and a half to 2 and a half inches across and are white, lavender, and purple with a conspicuous circular fringe. The flowering period extends from June to August.

The fruits ripen in August and September and are called maypops. They are oval to ellipsoid or almost round and 2 to 3 inches long. The smooth fleshy tissue is edible and becomes yellowish green to yellow when mature.

Another species, *P. lutea,* has a similar but smaller pale yellow to greenish flower and leaves with 3 rounded and shallowly cleft lobes having no marginal teeth.

Passion Flower, also called Maypops and Apricot Vine, grows in fields, roadsides, thickets, and sparse woods. It is an attractive and interesting, unusual vine that is easily grown from seeds or from cuttings.

Passion Flower

Passiflora incarnata

Passion Flower Family

Passifloraceae

Throughout most of the summer and autumn, dense clusters of tiny purple flowers develop at the tips of the exceedingly prickly stems. Striking in color and interesting in form, they bear a close resemblance to a single large flower and are frequently so mistaken. These floral clusters in time become converted into shining silvered heaps with the ripening and release of the brightly downy and buoyant fruits. The flowering and fruiting clusters, the stems, and the foliage are all thickly studded with sharp spines making thick colonies of this plant virtually impenetrable.

The stems are stout and 2 to 10 feet tall with conspicuous spiny wings that extend from one leaf to the other.

The large lobed and toothed leaves are as much as a foot in length with whitely hairy undersides and spines at the tips of all the lobes.

The very small pinkish purple flowers are crowded in rounded clusters about an inch in diameter with an enveloping base of prickly green bracts.

The diminutive fruits are less than one-sixth of an inch long with a tuft of delicate plumes an inch or more in length.

Three other species, *C. muticum, C. discolor, and C. altissimum,* have leaves with very white undersides. The first has no spines on the green base of the flowering head, and the second has very deeply cleft leaves. *C. pumilum* has a few flower heads 3 inches in diameter, and *C. arvense* has many flower heads an inch or less in diameter. *Carduus nutans* has large nodding heads.

Bull Thistle, or Common Thistle, grows in fields, roadsides, pastures, and meadows.

It is beauty and the beast rolled into one, a species with attractive flowering and fruiting, but it is also a powerfully aggressive weed. The handsome plumes making its fruits airborne also make it extremely difficult to control.

Bull Thistle

Composite Family

Cirsium vulgare

Compositae

Here is a plant attractive and interesting in flower, fruit, and foliage, yet the main reason for its popularity and widespread cultivation lies in the beauty and durability of one fragment of the fruit that remains long after the seeds have fallen.

The flattened rounded fruits are thin-walled, disklike pods about 2 inches long and nearly as broad. When the seeds have matured, the walls of the fruit separate and fall away leaving a silvery transparent or translucent membrane. There is little or no appreciable change in the appearance of these shimmering membranes from the time the fruits are mature in July on into the winter. In their persistence they remain as beauty spots after the flowers have all gone, and they are also used extensively for the enhancement of winter bouquets.

The height of the plant varies from 2 to 4 feet, and the branching stems have fairly large pointed leaves that are stalkless or have very short stalks. They are heart-shaped or triangular with coarse irregular teeth along the margins.

The flowering period is during May and June and usually produces an abundance of the fragrant, showy flowers that are almost an inch across and have large purple or pinkish purple petals.

Honesty has a long history of garden use in Europe and was introduced here for that purpose. It is said that the common name, Honesty, arises from the fact that through the thin walls of the fruits it can be seen that seeds have been set. The names Satin Flower, Moonwort, and Silver Dollar are also used.

This species can be easily propagated from seed in open or partially shaded sites. This is the manner in which it has escaped limitedly from cultivation to roadsides and fields.

Honesty

Lunaria annua

The spreading underground stems of this small herbaceous plant often provide extensive green colonies of ground cover for mountainous forest floors. From these underground organs are produced erect stems that are 2 to 8 inches tall and usually zigzag.

The nearly stalkless leaves are heart-shaped and taper gradually to a point. The lobes of the leaf base enclose the stem, so that it sometimes appears that the stem is growing through the leaf. There are generally only 2 leaves on a stem.

In May and June the very small white flowers appear in clusters about an inch long at the top of the stem. Although the individual flowers as well as the clusters are small, they are highly visible at the stem tip, and the dense colonies consist of a great number of plants at close quarters. The total picture then is that of a lush, thick, green carpet spread under the trees and embellished with many contrasting white spangles.

In late June and July the fallen flowers are replaced by the fruits that form and finally ripen during August and September. They are small berries that begin the process of maturation a grayish green that becomes speckled with dark brown or dull red dots.

This species is somewhat similar to False Solomon's Seal, *Smilacina racemosa,* as alluded to by the name Two-leaved Solomon's Seal, but the latter is a larger plant with many leaves and bright red fruits. Another name for this plant is Canada Mayflower.

Large colonies of Wild Lily of the Valley may be found in moist cool woods, and it is found at 6,000 feet elevation in the Great Smoky Mountains.

This low, creeping perennial herb is good cover for shaded and damp sites, and can be propagated by seed or underground stems.

Wild Lily of the Valley

Lily Family

Maianthemum canadense

Liliaceae

A small tree with a rounded crown of dark green foliage, it acquires an abundant sprinkling of luminous green patches at the time the fruits begin to develop in late summer. The color combination of these numerous areas of brightness figured upon the darker background of leaves brings about an interesting and attractive study in contrast.

The pale green fruiting structures strongly resemble those of the species of hop used commercially that imparts the bitter taste to beer. The fruits are formed as tiny nuts enclosed within flattened oval pouches that have a papery texture and are inflated. These pouches are pendulous from a long stalk in an elongated overlapping series.

This is a slender tree with furrowed brown bark that tends to scale off in narrow strips. It is usually not more than 30 feet tall, although it can reach a height of 50 feet or more. The slim branches are often gracefully inclined downward and display the beauty of the foliage to its best advantage.

The leaves are oval and pointed with very regular and sharply pointed teeth along the margins. They may be as much as 6 inches long and are a pale yellow in autumn.

Flowering takes place in April and May; and the flowers are minute. They are developed inconspicuously within a crowded succession of flattened scales. The male flowers are contained within scales that form a slender cylindrical tail.

Hop Hornbeam is also called American Hop Hornbeam, Eastern Hop Hornbeam, Leverwood, and Ironwood.

It grows in rich or low woods. The general form and foliage are attractive and are greatly enhanced by the fruits. Propagation is by seed sown in the fall.

Hop Hornbeam

Ostrya virginiana

Hazel Family

Corylaceae

P robably the fruits of this species are remembered more than the rest of the plant by those who travel the fields and woods, for the aftermath of any walk during fall or winter in their domain is the session devoted to removal of the "ticks."

This perennial herb produces two kinds of stems. One stem is no more than a foot tall and bears a cluster of leaves near the summit, while the other may be in excess of 3 feet and bears only flowers.

The leaves are divided into 3 ovate and pointed segments and are crowded at the apex of the shorter stem, while the flowers are usually deep pink to purple or sometimes white and grow in an elongated cluster at the top of the longer stem.

The fruits that develop from August to October consist of linear flat pods constricted at intervals into somewhat triangular segments that lend a sawtooth effect. The segments become separated later as the fruit matures and are covered with tiny hairs shaped like hooks. These hairs bind the segments to almost anything that makes contact with them and thus function in the dissemination of the seeds contained within.

There are several other species that are similar in flower, fruit, and leaf, but the leafless flowering stem of this species sets it apart from the others.

Other names have been applied to Beggar's Ticks that also refer to the sticky quality and to the 3-parted leaf such as Beggar Lice, Sticktights, Tick Trefoil, and Tick Clover.

All the species grow in wooded areas, and although looked upon generally as unwanted weeds, some of them, including this one, would be worthy of cultivation in partially shaded areas and have been so cited by some horticulturalists.

Beggar's Ticks

Desmodium nudiflorum

Pulse Family

Leguminosae

An herbaceous perennial about 2 or 3 feet tall, it does not ordinarily produce branches, and it has few leaves. The leaves, however, are large and are divided into many parts, thus giving the appearance of a greater content of branching and foliage. The small white flowers are not conspicuous as individuals, but their perch in a dense cluster at the tip of a long leafless stalk is a beacon marking the species in its shaded forest habitat.

It is late in the summer and on into autumn before the outstanding and unique feature that is the plant's namesake comes on the scene. The fruit of Doll's Eyes are indeed facsimiles of those structures used in the manufacture of dolls. The pattern of color and form of the fruiting arrangement is certainly one of the more striking wildflower displays.

The few large leaves are divided into several leaflets that are pointed and have margins that are toothed and lobed.

The flowers that are present in May and June have narrow petals and numerous stamens lending a tassel effect that is magnified by the many-flowered clusters.

The fruits are rounded berries nearly a half-inch across growing at the ends of thick red stalks. The color is usually white with a conspicuous black spot, but there is a form in which the white is replaced by red.

· Doll's Eyes is also known by the names White Cohosh and White Baneberry. The latter name refers to the fact that all parts of the plant are poisonous.

This species is found in rich woods, alluvial flood plains, and in wet thickets. The natural habitats of the plant are characteristically shady and moist, which suggests a good planting to brighten such plots of ground with attractive spring flowers and fall fruits, provided the plant's toxicity presents no problem. Seeds planted in fall or spring or division of roots in the spring can be used as propagation methods.

Doll's Eyes

Actaea pachypoda

Crowfoot Family

Ranunculaceae

The lustrous dark green leaves are pendant from the stems, flared near the tip, and frequently a foot in length. The appearance of the foliage imparts to this small tree an exotic mien, suggesting that the plant would be more at home in a tropical setting. The flowering period occurs in the early spring before the leaves develop and supplies an additional feature that further sets this species apart.

The flowers that bloom in April and May are unusual in color and form. They have two circles of three petals each arranged one inside the other, and their coloration ranges from green through several shades and combinations of purple and brown.

The fruits that develop and mature from August to October contribute yet another dimension of uniqueness. They resemble short, thickset bananas rounded at both ends and usually hanging from smooth stems in clusters of 2 or 4. Upon ripening their color progresses from green to yellow and brown. The sweet pulp is edible in the fall and has been described by some who favor it as custardlike and by others as bananalike. It has a spicy aroma when fully ripe and is marketed on a very limited basis.

There is one other species less common here. *A. parviflora* is a small shrub with smaller leaves, flowers, and fruits, but it is similar in form and color. It is found more to the east and south.

Other names that have been applied to this plant are Common Pawpaw, American Pawpaw, Tall Pawpaw, and Wild Banana Tree.

The environment in which the best growth occurs is that of rich moist woods. Pawpaw would introduce a touch of the tropics to such a site as it often forms dense thickets. It can be propagated by planting seeds sown in the autumn or by the planting of root cuttings.

Pawpaw
Asimina triloba

Custard-apple Family
Annonaceae

An unfortunately familiar Lorelei of the plant world, this ubiquitous vine can be extremely attractive and to some dangerously poisonous. The large 3-parted and deep green leaves present quite a winning summer foliage that changes in the autumn to varied shades of red that nicely set off the white to cream-colored clusters of fruits.

The stems may trail over the ground or climb into the tops of the tallest trees. Dense growths of small rootlets are produced along the stems giving the appearance of huge caterpillars, or millipedes.

The leaves consist of 3 oval, pointed leaflets 2 to 8 inches long having smooth or irregularly toothed margins. They may or may not be glossy.

Very small yellowish to greenish flowers develop in inconspicuous clusters 3 to 4 inches long during June and July.

In August and September the fruits mature as tiny berrylike spheres varying in color from white to yellowish gray or pale yellow. They are eaten by birds.

Poison Oak, *R. toxicodendron,* is very similar but shrubby with hairy fruits and more deeply lobed leaflets. Poison Sumac, *R. vernix,* is a large shrub or small tree with leaves of 7 or more smooth-margined leaflets. Fragrant Sumac, *R. aromatica,* is a nonpoisonous spicily fragrant shrub having leaves with regular rounded teeth and large clusters of red fruits.

Poison Ivy is also called Three-leaved Ivy, Mercury, Cow Itch, and Poison Oak. It is too plentiful practically everywhere but appears to do less well at higher elevations.

The chemical principle of the three toxic species is damaging not only to the skin but to the digestive tract if eaten and to the respiratory tract if breathed. Severe reactions have resulted in individuals working in the smoke of burning brush piles containing live or dead parts of these plants.

Poison Ivy

Rhus radicans

Cashew Family

Anacardiaceae

The heart-shaped leaves and triple-winged fruits of this perennial vine, carried upward by its climbing stems that twine about other plants, hang like ornaments from late summer through the autumn.

The aerial stems arise from enlarged underground stems and may grow to a length of 10 to 15 feet. These smooth stems climb by spiraling in a counterclockwise pattern.

The leaves grow singly on the stem as a rule; however, on the lower portion of the plant there may be one or more circles of leaves. The leaf shape is oval to heart-shaped with conspicuous veins radiating from the base of the blade.

The flowers that bloom in May and June are very small and white to greenish white or yellowish. They extend in slender pendant clusters from near the base of the leaf stalks.

The fruits begin to develop in June and continue on into November. At first green the color changes to a tan or light brown. The seeds are enclosed in a small capsule from which extend 3 semicircular wings about one-half to three-quarters of an inch long.

Cinnamon Vine, *D. batatas,* is a less common species with leaves somewhat similar to Wild Yam, except that they are in pairs and have 2 rounded lobes at the base of the blade. Fruits are rarely formed, but the plant produces aerial tubers that resemble small potatoes clustered at the base of the leaf stalks. It is interesting that Cinnamon Vine twines in clockwise fashion.

The term *yam* is commonly used for Sweet Potato, *Ipomoea batatas,* which is in the Morning Glory family.

Both these species are attractive vines that grow in moist woods and can be propagated by seeds, tubers, or cuttings.

Wild Yam
Dioscorea villosa

Yam Family
Dioscoreaceae

The tendency of this plant to grow in clumps combined with the development of profusely branched stems bearing an abundance of large leaves often produces thickets that are in effect walls of vegetation. The density of stems and foliage sometimes makes it difficult to observe interesting and unusual structures associated with fruiting.

This species is a shrub of medium size with somewhat hairy stems that attains a height of about 10 to 12 feet. The coarsely toothed leaves are broad and rounded at the base, sometimes lobed, and pointed at the tip.

The highly inconspicuous flowers appear in February and March long before any leaves are present. The inflorescences are in the form of short strings of brown scales within which are either male or female floral units of minute dimensions.

Toward the end of August and during September the fruits are maturing. An ovoid, pale brown or tan, hard-shelled nut is formed that is about one-half inch in diameter. Inside the hard shell is a sweet edible kernel. The fruit is enclosed within a rough and bristly pair of fused bracts, or leaves, shaped into a protrusion or beak about 2 inches long which has a frayed appearance at the tip.

There is another species, *C. americana,* that is very similar; however, the stems and leaf stalks are very hairy. The nut is also edible and about the same size but somewhat flattened, and the leafy covering does not form a beak.

The term *hazel* has been used in lieu of hazelnut, and the name *filbert* refers to the European hazelnut, *C. avellana.*

Both species here are found on roadsides, thickets, and fencerows. Nearly any kind of soil is satisfactory, and propagation is by seed or cuttings. The plants make an excellent hedge with an edible fruit.

Beaked Hazelnut

Corylus cornuta

Hazel Family

Corylaceae

Opening in April before the leaves have yet expanded to their full size, the flowers have good visibility. They are not large but are produced in great quantity and are attractive in their resemblance to small white bells hanging in long-stalked clusters from the ends of the stems.

When the leaves have completed their development, another dimension of beauty is added. The foliage is bright green and consists of large leaves with long stalks whose blades are divided into 3 oval or elliptic leaflets that taper abruptly to a point and have very finely toothed borders. This species is sometimes cultivated for use in ornamental planting primarily due to its handsome foliage.

The leaves and flowers both have appealing qualities; however, when the flowers begin to undergo the metamorphosis that shapes the fruiting structure, there appears still another interesting and embellishing feature. The fruiting forms that emerge are composed of 3 elongated, pale green lobes. Their thin walls have the texture of paper or parchment and are inflated. Light passing through the walls of these balloonlike fruits is suggestive of Japanese lanterns.

Bladdernut, or American Bladdernut, is a very thickly branched deciduous shrub, or small tree, that grows to a height of from 6 to 15 feet. The green-streaked branches bearing the 3-parted serrated leaves, the graceful pendant clusters of early flowers, and the distinctive lanternlike fruits that are prominent through the summer months and on into the fall all go to make a very attractive specimen.

Bladdernut grows in moist woods and thickets. It can be propagated by seeds or cuttings and grows in a variety of soils in moist and partially shaded situations.

Bladdernut

Staphylea trifolia

Bladdernut Family

Staphyleaceae

A deciduous tree with light gray bark and branches spreading into a broad crown, it may attain a height of 100 feet but is usually about 50 feet tall. The diameter of the trunk is generally 1 foot to 3 feet.

The large leaves measure a foot to over 2 feet in length. The blades of the leaves are divided into several pairs of leaflets arranged in rows. The leaflets are oval and tapered gradually to a point. Their margins are toothed, and their surfaces bear sticky hairs.

Flowering occurs during the month of May. The tiny flowers are rather inconspicuous; however, the males are produced in elongated clusters that show up as yellowish-green strings, or tails, 3 to 5 inches long.

The fruits that develop during the summer and ripen in September and October are quite conspicuous. The bright, yellowish-green husk is rounded and oblong with the ends often pointed, and the surface is covered with moist sticky hairs. The nut within has a rough, hard shell and contains an edible kernel.

There is another tree, *J. nigra,* somewhat similar in general form and appearance. It is a much more common species with much rougher and darker bark, and the fruits, also edible, are nearly spherical and lacking the clammy hairs.

The much lighter coloring of the bark of Butternut in comparison with *J. nigra* has resulted in another common name, White Walnut, being applied to this species. The sap is high in sugar content, and the trees have been tapped in the spring for syrup making. Fruit husks have been used as the source of a yellow dye.

Butternut inhabits rich moist woods. It is an attractive medium to large tree. It can be propagated by seeds that have been prevented from drying and planted in sandy soil. Transplantation of seedlings is best carried out when they are about two years old.

Butternut

Juglans cinerea

Walnut Family

Juglandaceae

The bright yellow and often red-tinted flowers of Witch Hazel appear at about the time its leaves have fallen. They sit upon the bare stems in small clusters that have a look of dishevelment from the curling and twisting of the narrow, ribbonlike petals. This is the time when other plants have ceased to flower. At this same time, curiously enough, the fruits from pollinations of the year past are just now ripening, and a mysterious crackling among the dry fallen leaves is explained by the explosive opening of the grayish brown and densely hairy capsules that propel the black seeds some distance from the plant. And it can be seen from leaves that may still hang onto the stems that the tissues of Witch Hazel respond to the injection of insect eggs by forming a gall that has the shape of a cone—or the hat of a witch. The exposed condition of the branches at this time of the year serves as a reminder of the mystique regarding the use of certain shapes and sizes of stems from particular portions of the plant as divining rods to reveal the location of water in the ground. It is now that the time of the celebration of Halloween is near.

Widely and irregularly branching stems may stand 20 feet tall to form a tall spreading shrub or straggling tree, and the large oval to nearly round leaves have scalloped margins and often asymmetrical bases.

Many kinds of preparations from all parts of the plant have been said to prevent or cure all manner of ailments. The American Indians, some of whom knew the species as Spotted Stick, used a boiled mixture of stems and leaves to control bleeding that was similar to the present day commercial product that has astringent properties.

Witch Hazel grows in moist or dry woods. It is an attractive shrub that provides flowers when they are a scarce commodity. Propagation is by seeds.

Witch Hazel

Hamamelis virginiana

Witch Hazel Family

Hamamelidaceae

Times of happiness, festive occasions, and general well-being are called to mind by mistletoe, for it is only during the Christmas season, when the plant is brought in for decoration, that it is really seen by most people. From far in the past this plant has been surrounded by a romantic and sentimental mystique now generally known only for its license to kiss a maid who stands beneath the mistletoe.

This small shrub is evergreen and stands only about a foot tall. The stems and leaves are green, and the leaves are wider and rounded at their tips. The species is partially parasitic upon the branches of trees, but, as indicated by its greenness, it synthesizes chlorophyll and thus manufactures its own food.

The small inconspicuous flowers develop in October and November and are greenish without petals. Mistletoe is also separate-sexed, so all the plants do not produce fruits.

From November to January the flowers that bear ovaries mature small white berries, each containing 2 to 3 seeds enveloped in a very sticky pulp. Birds feed on the berries and transport the adherent seeds to other trees.

The plant written about most as the traditional mistletoe is the European *Viscum album.* There are several other species in the United States, but the one closest to this area is the Dwarf Mistletoe, *Arceuthobium pusillum,* of New Jersey and Pennsylvania.

American Mistletoe is more common in the piedmont and coastal plain provinces. It lives on numerous species of deciduous trees, and in those instances in which heavy infestation has occurred there is evident and sometimes gross deformation of the branches.

Mistletoe is not known to be cultivated.

American Mistletoe

Mistletoe Family

Phoradendron flavescens

Loranthaceae

In April or May, before the leaves make their appearance, the naked stems are populated by numerous dense clusters of very small, pale yellow flowers. The plant is usually thickly branched in either an erect or straggling pattern and is ordinarily no more than 6 feet tall. The stems and the leaves give off an aromatic fragrance when bruised.

Soon after the flowering, the stems are clothed with 3-parted leaves. Each of the 3 oval segments has irregularly toothed or scalloped margins.

Beginning in June or July, the flowers are replaced by compact bunches of rounded, berrylike fruits that have a bearded appearance due to their close covering of bristly hairs. Their red to orange-red color is persistent on into the fall.

The leaves of Fragrant Sumac, or Sweet Scented Sumac, are somewhat similar to those of another member of this genus, *R. radicans,* Poison Ivy. The poisonous plant has greenish white flowers in June and July, white fruits, and its terminal, or middle, leaf segment has a long stalk.

Fragrant Sumac is an attractive little shrub with a procession of favorable characteristics to recommend it. In the early spring its yellow flowered stems are conspicuous, and the deep green and light-veined tripartite leaves are desirable in color and form. The colorful and distinctively hairy fruits come in early and stay late, and there is a red and orange autumnal foliage finale. All this and a spicy aroma too.

This plant grows in dry open woods, on roadside banks and wood borders, and on rocky slopes. It can be propagated by seeds sown in the fall or by root cuttings; it does well in a wide range of soils in a sunny site. It is particularly suited to rocky soils.

Fragrant Sumac

Rhus aromatica

Cashew Family

Anacardiaceae

Long after the procession of floral brightness has passed and beyond the transition time of the varied hues of autumnal foliage there remain oases of color punctuating the bleakness of the winter months wherever barberry grows. The lustrous scarlet berries retain their brilliance very nearly until spring.

The densely branched and thorny stems produce a broad, full shrub reaching a height of about 4 to 7 feet. The small, bright green leaves are smooth on the margins and wider and rounded at the tip. The color of the leaves becomes a deep red in the fall. Just beneath each cluster of leaves there protrudes a straight slender thorn.

During April and May there is a profusion of small yellow flowers that have an interesting trait. The stamens are sensitive to touch and when stimulated spring toward the center of the flower, whereby any visiting insect is showered with pollen. This behavior may be observed by gently moving a slender straw around within the flower.

During the latter part of the summer and early fall there is a transformation from green and yellow to scarlet brought about by the ripening of an abundant crop of bright fruits about half an inch long.

This species was introduced from Japan for purposes of ornamental planting but has escaped from cultivation and established itself here. Another species, *B. canadensis,* has somewhat similar flowers and fruits, but the margins of the leaves are toothed, and the thorns are branched.

Japanese Barberry is found wild in open woods, pastures, and roadsides. It makes an excellent low hedge and is very hardy. Propagation can be carried out from green cuttings, and germination from seeds occurs readily. Planting is best done in a light, well-drained loam.

Japanese Barberry

Berberis thunbergii

Barberry Family

Berberidaceae

Growth usually takes the form of a tangled mass of stems often 3 or 4 feet long, some erect and some prostrate or leaning on other nearby plants. A closer look at this jumble reveals some interesting and attractive features.

The stems are square, and the angles are equipped with stiff bristles that are curved downward toward the base of the plant. These bristles can be easily demonstrated by running one's fingers up the stem or by pulling the stem across an article of clothing.

The arrangement of the leaves on the stem resembles a series of small wheels on an axle. There are generally 8 leaves that encircle the stem at the same level, and these leaves, like the stems, have bristles directed toward their bases.

From May to July small clusters of tiny white flowers develop on stalks growing from the angle between the leaves and the stem. Although the inflorescence is never conspicuous, the stem, leaf, and floral structures together fashion a delicate composite.

At the onset of fruiting the ovary of each flower produces a pair of diminutive spherical fruits that are beset with hooked bristles. From summer into autumn the fruit color changes from green to pink to brown or black.

The bristly display almost insures that the plant will cling to objects contacting it, whence came the name Cleavers. The names Bedstraw and Goosegrass arose from use as bedding and as food for geese.

There are several somewhat similar mountainous species of *Galium,* but the bristly character and number of leaves in a circle identify Cleavers.

This plant grows well in shady woods or on open roadsides. Although very tolerant it is not ordinarily suitable for planting except as a curiosity.

Cleavers

Galium aparine

Madder Family

Rubiaceae

This herbaceous perennial is seen in the spring as a solitary greenish white flower between two veiny and crinkled leaves as yet unexpanded. The lone flower is small and has no petals, so there is little in the way of floral display. The floral parts do, however, include several pistils, each of which produces a darkly red berry. By late summer the red clusters of berries are quite striking, and the leaves beneath have developed to several times their size at the time when flowering first occurred.

The plant grows from a yellow underground stem, or rhizome, to a height of a few inches to nearly 2 feet. The aerial stem usually has 2 leaves below the flower and one more leaf from the base of the plant.

The leaves are broadly heart-shaped in general outline, and their width is frequently equal to or in excess of their length. There are usually 5 to 7 lobes with toothed margins. The leaves are long-stalked, and at maturity they may well measure 8 to 10 inches across.

The flower opens in April and May and is borne upon a long, hairy, and leafless stalk. The flower parts consist essentially of numerous slender stamens and pistils without any petals. The appearance is that of a small greenish white tassel.

The fruits are mature in July as a fused cluster of berries about one-half inch in diameter. Each berry is ellipsoidal and tipped with a curved pointed beak.

Golden Seal is also known as Yellow Root and "Tumeric." The name *Yellow Root* refers to the yellow underground stem for which the plant has been so heavily harvested to be sold as a medicinal that severe depopulation of the species has resulted. Golden Seal grows in rich woods and is an attractive little herb that can be grown from seeds which could be instrumental in establishing new footholds.

Golden Seal

Hydrastis canadensis

Crowfoot Family

Ranunculaceae

One of the first trees to raise a floral flag of spring, Serviceberry is one of those welcome plants that are among the early reminders of winter's end. It then continues on to unfold a series of appealing features.

This small tree, usually less than 30 feet tall, is sometime shrubby. The stems have smooth gray bark and tend to branch in a somewhat clustered pattern that produces a slender crown.

The oblong leaves have rounded bases and pointed tips with small teeth on the margins. The leaves do not expand until after the flowers have opened.

From as early as late March through June the flowers appear and clothe the bare stems in a cloud of white, ribbon-like petals that hang in nodding clusters. Most trees are so heavily flowered that practically every branch is traced as if by snowfall.

The fruits that develop and ripen from June through August resemble small apples. They are about one-half-inch across and red to reddish purple. Many animals use these edible fruits as food.

Another species, *A. sanguinea,* is much less common and has much more rounded to nearly circular leaves. It is present more in the northern Blue Ridge Mountains.

Serviceberry is also known as Common Serviceberry, Service Tree, Sarviceberry, Sarvis Tree, Sarvis, Shadbush, Juneberry, and Sugarplum. The stories that go with the origin of plant names are oftentimes quite interesting. This species is found growing from the mountains to the coast. For people who were unable to survive the winter cold of the mountains, there were services, and this plant was in flower. On the coast in the early spring the anadromous shad were running, and this plant was in flower.

Serviceberry can be grown from seeds that are planted in the fall.

Serviceberry
Amelanchier arborea

Rose Family
Rosaceae

Forest floors are frequently furnished, even in winter, with variegated green carpets that in spring and summer become dappled with red and white wherever this evergreen herb is established.

The low-growing stems trail along the ground oftentimes forming spreading mats of very lush growth. The leaves are arranged in pairs along the stem and are oval to nearly round. Leaf color may be uniformly green, but more often there are lines of pale or yellowish green to almost white following along the pattern of veins.

With May and June comes a spray of white flowers, their interiors set with soft hairs. In some plants the style, or centerpiece, of the flower protrudes, while the stamens or pollen-bearing structures are included within the petals. In other plants just the reverse is true. The flowers grow in pairs, and the basal portions of the pair are fused together. Sometimes all parts of the pair are fused.

The advent of June and July is accompanied by the development of the fruits. The fruits produced are bright red berries that remain relatively unchanged almost throughout the winter. Infrequently a white berry is formed.

The developmental process of fruiting is unusual in that the ovaries of two flowers are fused and yield a double berry. The evidence of this dual production can usually be detected by examination of the ends of the berry.

Birds and other animals eat the berries, and a tea prepared from them has been said to be beneficial as an aid during the birth process.

Other names that have been given to Partridge Berry are Two-eyed-berry, Running Box, Checkerberry, and Squaw-berry.

This plant is found in moist or relatively dry woods and does well if divided into several small mats and planted in partially shaded areas.

Partridge Berry

Mitchella repens

Madder Family

Rubiaceae

The long stout stems bristle with a scattering of slender spines hidden in a dense growth of purplish red hairs. They extend for 6 feet or more in a graceful arching fashion and frequently bring forth new shoots where their recurving tips touch the ground and take root.

The tripartite leaves are composed of 3 oval, pointed leaflets that have toothed margins and are covered with a thick growth of white hairs underneath.

The basal lobes of the flowers that appear in May and June are tapered to slender points and together resemble a star at the center of which the much shorter white petals sit.

The fruits, which mature from July to September, are about one-half-inch across. Their color is a lustrous red, and they are juicy and edible. There is a slight depression at the point where the fruit separated from the flower.

There are two other species, *R. odoratus* and *R. idaeus,* with red fruits, but the former has purple flowers and its leaves are not divided into three parts, while the latter's fruits are hairy.

Wineberry has also been given the name Wine Raspberry. Its home countries are Korea, Japan, and China, but it has escaped from cultivation and has become established in this country.

The curving growth pattern of the branches combines with their reddish purple bristliness and the two-toned quality of the leaves, green above and white below, to produce a most handsome display of vegetative features. And to this is added the high color and edibility of the fruits that mark this as an attractive and useful ornamental plant.

It is found growing in many open woods, roadside banks, wood borders, and fencerows.

Wineberry

Rubus phoenicolasius

Rose Family

Rosaceae

This is one of the showiest of shrubs during the time its fruits are ripening. The flowers and foliage are both attractive features of the plant, but the combination of color and size of the fruit clusters is outstanding.

The stout stems generally reach a height of 8 to 10 feet, but they are sometimes much taller. They tend to be straight, and the surface is dotted with conspicuous wartlike growths. Stems and leaves that become bruised give off a disagreeable odor.

The leaves grow in pairs on the stem and are usually spaced well apart. Their blades are divided into several graceful leaflets that have toothed margins and taper gradually to a slender point.

The flowers bloom in April and May and are small but occur in large numbers. A great many dense clusters of white to cream-colored flowers are produced in the form of an oval or sphere.

The fruiting period of June to August brings a transfiguration of these floral clusters into mounds of tightly packed berries of the brightest scarlet. Several species of birds feed on these berries.

Common Elder, *S. canadensis,* is a more common species that is similar in stem and leaf, but the flowering and fruiting clusters are flat-topped, and the fruits are deep purple or black.

Red-berried Elder, also called by the names Red Elderberry and Stinking Elder, is poisonous in all parts. Both the straight stems, hollowed out to make peashooters, and the berries have caused poisoning in children.

Red-berried Elder is found in rocky woods and clearings at higher elevations. It is a fine addition to sites with rich soil, for its handsome foliage, early flowering, and especially for its brilliant fruits, but remember the toxicity. Propagation can be carried out by seeds and by stem or root cuttings.

Red-berried Elder

Honeysuckle Family

Sambucus pubens

Caprifoliaceae

Old fields, roadsides, and the borders of woodlands in early to middle summer are often beautified by the presence of thick colonies of shrubs that in some measure have the countenance of giant ferns. The stalks of their large and long leaves are reddish purple, and the blades are made up of many slender leaflets that show flashes of gleaming white when their undersides are turned in the breezes. Above the leaves wave the sizable pyramids of greenish yellow and fragrant flowers that are usually a-buzz with their many insect pollinators.

Late summer and autumn present the most striking phase of the life cycle of this plant. The handsome foliage is now accompanied by the torches of densely clustered deep red fruits, and the leaves attain a scarlet brilliance. The resulting combination of color and form produces an effect of exotic beauty.

The smooth, purplish brown stems usually stand 3 to 15 feet tall with the long leaves borne in a radiating pattern. The leaflets are toothed and sharp-pointed, arranged in 2 rows on the leaf stalks.

Flowers and fruits are very small and grow in clusters 4 to 10 inches long. Flowering is in June and July, and the fruits ripen from August until October. The fruits are persistent on into the winter months.

Two other species, *R. typhina* and *R. copallina,* are easily identified by the velvety hairs of stems and leaf stalks in the former and the wings extending between the leaflets in the latter.

Smooth Sumac, also called Common Sumac, has had its fruits used to make a beverage and its stems chewed to prevent dental caries and oral infections.

It is found in almost any dry sunny locations and is a handsome addition to exposed grounds especially when grown in colonies, and the fruits remain nearly unchanged through winter. Propagation is accomplished by seeds or root cuttings.

74

Smooth Sumac

Cashew Family

Rhus glabra

Anacardiaceae

Leaves, flowers, and fruits appear to be the only component parts of this low-growing herb. The apparent stemlessness results from one of its stems, a rhizome, being underground and the other, a runner, being very slender and prostrate. When in fruit it looks a lot like Wild Strawberry or a smaller edition of Garden Strawberry, but in flower it resembles Cinquefoil, or Five Finger.

The leaves have very long stalks, and the blades are divided into 3 oval segments bordered with small rounded teeth.

The flowers are yellow and have long slender stalks. Just below the base of the flower there are 5 bracts each having 3 teeth at their tip. These bracts are useful identifying features of the species.

There is a great deal of similarity in the appearance of the fruits of this plant and those of the true strawberry, but the taste is totally dissimilar as the Indian Strawberry fruits are dry and essentially tasteless.

Wild Strawberry, *Fragaria virginiana,* is similar in general appearance but has white flowers and delicious fruits and is one of the parents of Garden Strawberry, *F. ananassa,* which is larger in all parts.

Both *Potentilla canadensis* and *P. simplex,* Cinquefoil, or Five Finger, which bear some likeness to Indian Strawberry, have leaves divided into 5 segments, no red fruit, and lack the 3-toothed bracts beneath the flower.

Indian Strawberry is an introduction from Asia that is also called by the names Mock Strawberry, Snake Strawberry, and Yellow Strawberry.

It is a perennial herb that becomes established in open moist woods, lawns, roadsides, and pastures.

Indian Strawberry

Duchesnea indica

Rose Family

Rosaceae

The unique floral architecture of this species lends a distinctiveness that makes identification an easy matter. There, however is a wide range of variability particularly with respect to size and pigmentation. The plant may grow 6 inches tall, or it may surpass 3 feet. "Jack," a fleshy stalk from which the tiny flowers grow, and the "pulpit," a leafy hood curving over him, may be white, green, brown, or purple, and the hood may be solid or striped.

There may be a single leaf or 2 leaves on long stalks, consisting of 3 large, pointed leaflets that are sometimes nearly a foot long.

The intriguing beauty of these hooded plants standing monklike in the quiet shady places where they grow is in sharp contrast to the fire of fruiting that follows. The subdued tones of the flowering period from April to June are replaced in July by the vivid hues revealed as the large clusters of lustrous berries change from green to orange to scarlet.

The stem of the plant is underground and, like all the other parts, contains calcium oxalate crystals that produce a stinging sensation in the mouth or throat. After being cooked the stem is edible and was used as food by the American Indians.

A somewhat similar but much less common species, *A. dracontium,* has a single leaf that is divided into 7 or more leaflets and a very slender elongated flowering stalk that protrudes far beyond the hood. In this case Jack is much too tall for the pulpit.

Jack-in-the-pulpit, also known as Indian Turnip and Dragon Arum, thrives in moist woods, bogs, and swamps frequently forming extensive, dense colonies.

This is an interesting and attractive perennial herb that makes a good conversation piece for wildflower gardens and provides some bright color in late summer. It can be propagated by planting the underground stems or seeds.

Jack-in-the-pulpit

Arum Family

Arisaema triphyllum

Araceae

This deciduous tree usually develops a pyramidal crown that stands about 40 to 70 feet high but sometimes reaches 90 feet. The straight trunk extends nearly to the top of the crown producing slender branches with smooth young stems that are a lustrous reddish brown. In winter these stems are tipped with large buds enclosed in silvery hairs.

The large broad leaves taper gradually or abruptly to a point and measure 4 to 12 inches in length. They are scattered along the stems.

The flowering period is in May and June and produces flowers of good size and interesting form, but they tend to blend with the colors of the stems and leaves. The central greenish pistils and numerous orange-yellow stamens are inclosed by 6 erect petals that are 2 to 3 inches long and yellow to greenish or bluish yellow.

The development of fruits in August and September produces a green, conelike structure about 2 to 4 inches long somewhat resembling a cucumber. On ripening the color changes from green to dark red or purplish red. Every now and then alterations in the plans for fruit development occur, resulting in deviations that produce exotic architectural curiosities.

Other species of magnolias have white flowers but are fairly similar in leaf, flower, and fruit. *M. tripetala* has leaves 1 to 2 feet long that are clustered at the stem tips. The leaves of *M. fraseri* have earlike lobes at the base. One rare species, *M. macrophylla,* possess leaves a foot to a yard long. *M. virginiana,* usually a more coastal species, has small leaves much whitened beneath, and *M. grandiflora* has tough and leathery evergreen leaves.

Cucumber Tree, also called Cucumber Magnolia, inhabits rich woods. It is an attractive tree in form and foliage and interesting in its colorful and sometimes oddly formed fruits. Propagation is by seed with planting in rich soil.

Cucumber Tree

Magnolia Family

Magnolia acuminata

Magnoliaceae

Honeysuckles comprise some of the handsomest ornamental shrubs and vines of our flora, and this species has as much to recommend it as any other member of the group. It is a shrub of medium to large size with a spreading habit and a thickly branched pattern of stems that display the lush dark green foliage. On this rich, leafy backdrop the development of showy flowers and glossy fruits contribute to a procession of attractive forms and colors.

The dark, short-stalked leaves are arranged in pairs and are oblong or ovate with the ends rounded or blunt-pointed. The dark green upper surface has a roughened or wrinkled appearance contrasted with the grayish lower surface, which is softly hairy.

The flowers come in May and June and usually in large numbers. They are at first white, and as they age the color changes to yellow or yellowish tan. The flowers are colorful and abundant with the pigment change adding another two-toned dimension, but a beauty of a different form and hue rivaling that of the floral display materializes when the fruits mature.

The fruit is a shining berry approximately one-quarter inch in diameter that is usually blood-red, but occasionally a plant will produce yellow to orange berries that are remindful of miniature pumpkins. Whatever the color, it is strong and lustrous, and since heavy fruiting is a mark of this species, July and August usher in this deep green shrubbery densely spangled with red or orange.

Morrow's Honeysuckle is a native of Japan that has escaped cultivation as an ornamental and become naturalized.

The plant can be propagated by seed sown in the fall. Planting would have to be in a location where growth of a broad shrub could be accommodated.

Morrow's Honeysuckle

Lonicera morrowi

Honeysuckle Family

Caprifoliaceae

Throughout the summer and into the fall the rich floral purple and yellow, the handsome dark green foliage, and the berries in transit from green to orange and crimson are all presented together. This array of vivid and contrasting colors may be seen trailing along the ground or hanging from the taller surrounding vegetation.

The stems of this attractive vine may scramble over the lower plants or climb by twining about the stems of shrubs or trees often to a height of 10 or 12 feet. The older portions of the stem nearer the ground are woody.

Generally, oval or heart-shaped, the leaves usually have a pair of lobes at the base of the blade so deeply cut that they frequently give the appearance of three separate leaves. Bruising of the leaves produces a disagreeable odor.

Flowering begins in June and continues into September. The bright yellow stamens form a cone that projects from the center of each flower, and encircling the base of this cone are 5 backswept deep purple petals that taper gradually to a point. The effect is that of a golden shooting star leaving a purple wake.

Fruiting commences not long after the flowers open, and the fruits develop and ripen all through the season. These oval crimson berries are about a half-inch long and are displayed in glistening clusters that add their changing colors of maturation to that of the newly developing flowers.

Other names for Nightshade are Climbing Nightshade, Woody Nightshade, and Bittersweet.

This plant is a European introduction that has become established along roadsides, wood borders, and in moist thickets and streamsides.

Nightshade is an ornamental plant in foliage, flower, and fruit, but it is poisonous, and the colorful berries are a dangerous attraction for children.

Nightshade

Solanum dulcamara

Nightshade Family

Solanaceae

Conformation, foliage, flowers, and fruits compete strongly for ornamental honors in this species. The overall appearance of the plant is exceptionally attractive, and so it is with each of its component parts.

This is a shrub that grows to a height of 2 to 10 feet. There is frequent branching that produces some unusual and interesting shapes formed by the long and spreading stems that often curve downward. The bark is light brown, and much of it on the older stems peels off in slender strips, but not necessarily in nine strips as the name specifies.

The handsome foliage consists of dark green leaves that are highly variable in form. Some of the leaves have 3 distinct lobes with evenly spaced marginal teeth, while others are very irregularly lobed and toothed.

The purple-stamened white, or occasionally pinkish, flowers are pretty but only about one-half-inch across; they occur in very dense clusters that are nearly spherical and about 2 inches across. These showy clusters appear in large numbers throughout the plant from May to July.

The fruits that begin to form shortly after the flowering period continue to develop until September and are persistent far on into the winter. From each flower there arises a group of from 3 to 5 oval, pointed pods that are somewhat the shape of a teardrop. As the fruits mature they take on several coloration combinations of pink, purple, and brown. They have a papery texture and appear swollen or inflated.

Ninebark is found in moist thickets and on moist rocky slopes. It grows especially well in sandy or rocky soil near water.

It is sometimes cultivated for use as shrubbery or as single plantings. It can be propagated by either seeds or cuttings.

Ninebark

Physocarpus opulifolius

Rose Family

Rosaceae

The lush, handsome foliage is of fine color and form and is beautifully displayed on a system of branches that fashions a full rounded symmetry, but the best is yet to come, for the months of autumn bring a shower of multicolored and highly complementary fruit clusters.

The plant is characterized by very rapid growth that usually produces a tree of medium size, though larger specimens do occur. The pattern of stem growth often results in a tree that is almost circular in silhouette.

The leaves are composed of many oval, pointed segments arranged in pairs along a stalk that is often over 2 feet long. This combination of size and composition is fernlike and is responsible for the exotic effect produced by this plant.

The green or greenish yellow flowers appear in June and July. The individual flower is small, but large numbers of clusters are formed, and many of these measure well over a foot in length. Male flowers have an unpleasant odor, so trees with female flowers are more attractive during the flowering period.

Beginning during July and continuing on into October, the hosts of small yellow flowers are converted to bunches of flattened papery fruits with a single seed in the center. These fruits are generally twisted and pointed at both ends, and color changes include pale green, pink, rust, purplish red, copper, bronze, and tan.

Tree of Heaven is native to China and has escaped cultivation here as an ornamental. It has also been named Copal Tree and Paradise. It is found on roadsides and in fields and does well in some of the worst soils. It can be propagated from seed, or better yet, from basal shoots from female trees.

Tree of Heaven

Ailanthus altissima

Quassia Family

Simaroubaceae

The array of bright red berries of autumn and their enveloping mist of finely divided greenery originated from the fleshy young shoots that appeared in the early spring. These shoots might have been harvested and eaten, for the plant that grows in the wild is the same species that is cultivated for the commercial asparagus spears.

Growth of the green stem results in progressively smaller branches that terminate in numerous clusters of threadlike branchlets imparting a fernlike aspect.

The delicate green branchlets function as leaves and are frequently mistaken for them, but the true leaves are small, colorless, scalelike structures at the bases of the stems. The true leaves are relatively large and conspicuous on the young shoots.

The small, bell-shaped flowers that appear in May and June are greenish or yellowish and have low visibility in the rich green cloud of slender stems.

From July to October the fruits mature as brilliant red berries about one-third of an inch in diameter. Plants are frequently heavily fruited and are quite showy.

Extracts have been used as a tonic and as a remedy for toothache, and the roasted seeds have been used as substitutes for coffee.

Asparagus was introduced from Europe for cultivation as food and also has the name Garden Asparagus, since other exotic species have been introduced for use as ornamentals in sprays and bouquets and are referred to as asparagus "ferns."

This herbaceous perennial inhabits fields, roadsides, and open woods. It is easily grown from seed in almost any kind of soil; however, planting for food is best done with proper spacing, soil conditioning, and fertilization.

Asparagus

Asparagus officinalis

Lily Family

Liliaceae

Toward the end of spring and the beginning of summer, one of the most impressive plants of the forests is the Black Locust. Pendulous strings of fragrant white flowers hang in profusion among the many-parted leaves. When summer is about through, the fruits are maturing and by autumn have ripened into clusters of brown to red-purple pods.

This tree reaches a height of 60 to 80 feet and has relatively short branches that form an irregularly slender crown. At the base of the leaf stalks there is a pair of short sharp spines. The dark brown bark is deeply furrowed producing long vertical ridges.

The leaves are 8 inches to a foot long and have blades composed of several pairs of oval leaflets arranged in 2 rows with a single leaflet at the tip.

The flowers bloom in May and June and develop in slender clusters 2 to 4 inches long. Each flower is an inch or less long and is similar in form to those of pea or clover. The base is yellowish brown, and the petals are a creamy white.

The fruits ripen in September and October as smooth, flattened pods 2 to 4 inches long. The color ranges from light to dark brown or rust as a rule, but often a striking dark red to reddish purple pod appears.

Another member of the genus, *R. hispida,* is somewhat similar in leaf and flower shape, but this species is a shrub that has pink to purple flowers and rough hairy pods.

Black Locust, also known as False Acacia, grows in open woods, fields, and roadsides, so it does well in almost any soil and tolerates heat and drought. It grows readily from seeds, and the young plants develop rapidly. It has something for all seasons and could be used as an ornamental more than it is.

Black Locust

Robinia pseudo-acacia

Pulse Family

Leguminosae

The raspberries and blackberries are very similar plants. All the other species in this area are characterized by prickly stems and leaves with the blades divided into several parts. Purple-flowering Raspberry possess neither of these features. Its stems are hairy but prickleless, and the leaf blades are in one piece that is more like maple. And for good measure the flower is strongly remindful of that of a rose.

It is a spreading shrub 3 to 6 feet tall with unarmed stems that branch widely and tend to arch. The bark of the older stems peels off in thin strips.

The leaves are 4 to 8 inches long and wide, consisting of from 3 to 5 pointed lobes with irregularly toothed margins.

The long flowering period extends from June through August. The flowers are fragrant and measure about 2 inches across. The base of the flower and the flower stalks are densely covered with red hairs, while the rounded petals are pinkish purple. The similarity to wild roses is striking.

The fruits ripen over the period from middle to late July on through September or until frost. They are hemispherical and red to purple with a diameter of approximately one-half to three-quarters of an inch. There is some difference of opinion as to their edibility. Reports of dryness, juiciness, palatability, and unpalatability have been made.

Purple-flowering Raspberry is also known by the names Flowering Raspberry and Thimbleberry.

This shrub is found along wood borders and moist roadside banks, on rocky slopes, and in stream valleys.

It grows very nicely in shaded situations and spreads rapidly. The combined qualities of its affinity for shaded and rocky sites along with the ornamental values are notable. Propagation is by seeds or root cuttings.

Purple-flowering Raspberry

Rose Family

Rubus odoratus

Rosaceae

Commonly 3 to 10 feet tall, this spreading shrub sometimes attains a much greater height. Its widely branching smooth stems are seen as reddish glints among the rich foliage. The large, dark green leaves are smooth and glossy providing a highly complementary backdrop for the fragrant white spheres of flowers of summer. Late in summer and in the autumn the progress of fruiting is marked by a shifting of pigments from the white of the floral clusters to the purplish red or russet of the fruiting balls.

The beauty of pond margins and stream banks is often enhanced by the shining foliage and dense flower clusters. The oval and pointed leaves, many of them 6 to 8 inches long, are arranged in pairs or occasionally in circles of 3 to 4, and the densely compacted small tubular flowers with their long protruding styles give an attractive pincushion effect. The flowers bloom from June to August, and the fruits begin development in August with final ripening coming in September or October.

The tightly clustered and very small fruits are about one-quarter-inch long and conical in shape with their attachment at the point of the cone. The aggregate of fruits measures almost an inch in diameter. The immature fruits are a light green that becomes tinted with purplish red and finally brown.

Buttonbush is also called Honey Balls and Globeflower. Its fruits are a source of food for species of wildlife, and preparations of the bark have been used to reduce the pain of toothache.

It is found on the edges of ponds and lakes, in swamps, and along streambanks.

Buttonbush is a handsome shrub that grows well in moist sandy soil, and it can be propagated from seeds or cuttings.

Buttonbush

Cephalanthus occidentalis

Madder Family

Rubiaceae

This deciduous shrub branches widely from ground level to produce a profusion of spreading stems that are oftentimes spiny and may attain a height of 10 to 12 feet. The plant at times may appear to take on a somewhat metallic cast from sunlight playing on the silvery scales that are formed on the young stems and other parts of this species.

The stems bear a dense crop of oval, pointed leaves that are about 1 to 3 inches long and coated on the undersides with silver scales.

In May and June clusters of fragrant white to yellowish white flowers bloom. These are in the form of a slender tube flared at the tip and covered with silver scales.

The most conspicuous and colorful phase of the plant's cycle comes in the late summer and autumn when the fruits develop. They are pink to red ovals approximately a half-inch long and spangled with the silver scales.

A less common species, *E. pungens,* is similar to Autumn Olive but is evergreen with slightly larger leaves and fruits and reddish brown scales on the leaf undersides.

Autumn Olive, also called Silverberry, is an Asiatic introduction that has escaped cultivation and become established here. It is a species that is extensively planted to provide shelter and food for wildlife. It is from these many plantings that the plant has escaped and become established along roadsides, in fencerows, and in low woods.

Besides its use for wildlife, this shrub is ornamental with respect to foliage, flower, and fruit. It is attractive as a single planting, and it also makes an excellent hedge.

It can be grown from seed stored in alternating layers of soil until the second year or from cuttings. Planting should be in a sunny, well-drained site.

Autumn Olive

Oleaster Family

Elaeagnus umbellata

Elaeagnaceae

On a warm day with a little breeze in the air, Spicebush is likely to be detected before it is seen. The entire plant gives off an aromatic fragrance resembling the scent of lemon. In the early spring its numerous slender limbs bear countless clusters of small yellow flowers in conspicuous display, since no leaves have yet appeared. A short time later, when leafing has occurred, the branches are hidden by a thick growth of spicy, bright green foliage that undergoes an autumnal transformation to a bright yellow. The autumn also brings with it the culmination of fruiting, which leaves the stems studded with gems of vivid glossy red.

This is a deciduous shrub of many smooth and slender branches that is commonly 4 to 15 feet tall. Bruised or broken stems release a strong and spicy perfume.

The thin smooth leaves are about 2 to 5 inches long. They are oval to oblong and pointed at both ends with the widest part frequently nearer the tip.

The very small flowers are bright yellow and fragrant and are produced in numerous dense clusters on the naked stems from March to May.

Oval to oblong and sparkling red, the fruits that mature in August and September resemble berries one-forth to one-half inch long.

More names for Spicebush are Benjamin Bush, Wild All-spice, and Fever Bush. Its leaves and fruits have been used as a flavoring in foods and in the making of spicy tealike beverages. The fruits are eaten by several species of birds, and the bark and stems were steeped to prepare fever remedies.

It is found along stream banks and in rich moist woodlands. An ornamental shrub for planting in partially shaded sites, it offers an early floral display and closes the season with brilliant fruit color while providing fragrant foliage throughout. Propagation is easily effected by seeds or transplantation.

Spicebush

Lindera benzoin

Lauraceae

The arching and leafy stems of this very common perennial herbaceous species contribute to the spring flowering season with many-flowered white plumes at their tips. By the time the spring festivities have been replaced by autumn the process of fruiting has exchanged the white floral clusters with ones of red.

The unbranched stems arise from large underground rhizomes and ascend to a height of a foot to more than 3 feet. They are usually curved and often somewhat zigzag and are practically hidden from view by the many broad leaves.

The large leaves are spread horizontally in 2 rows along the stem. Their pointed blades are shallowly furrowed lengthwise and wider near the middle. The overall length ranges from 4 to 10 inches.

Extremely small greenish white to white flowers form a large cluster at the apex of the stem during May and June. The cluster is usually open and full but can be rather slender.

The fruits that develop during August to October are red berries about one-quarter inch in diameter. It is interesting that they develop a fine stippling of brownish to purplish red specks closely resembling the maturation of fruits in *Maianthemum canadense,* which is called Two-leaved Solomon Seal.

Solomon's Seal, *Polygonatum biflorum,* is a fairly similar species, but its flowers and blue or black berries hang from the underside of the stem.

False Solomon's Seal is called by several other names, among them are False Spikenard, Solomon's Plume, Solomon's Zigzag, and Plumelily.

It is spread throughout the area in moist woods and sometimes on moist roadside embankments.

This plant is ornamental in foliage, flower, and fruit and grows well in any good soil in partially shaded sites. Propagation is by rhizome cuttings.

False Solomon's Seal

Lily Family

Smilacina racemosa

Liliaceae

The few divided leaves of Ginseng give the appearance of a plant possessing freely branching and thickly leaved stems. The foliage is handsome and far excels the small dull flowers in both beauty and conspicuousness. When autumn arrives, however, and the shining red cluster of berries ripens, this plant then becomes one of the brightest spots in the woodlands.

From the large, spindle-shaped, and often forked root, a single straight and unbranched stem grows to a height of as much as 2 feet.

Three or 4 long-stalked leaves encircle the stem. Each leaf consists of usually 5 stalked and radiating leaflets having toothed margins and pointed tips.

The small white to greenish white flowers appear in June and July and are arranged in a stalked, rounded cluster that arises from the end of the stem.

The brilliant red berries form a compact sphere centrally situated within the circle of leaves. Each berry is nearly half an inch in diameter.

Dwarf Ginseng, *P. trifolius,* is a very rare species that has a spherical root, leaflets without stalks, and yellow fruits.

Ginseng, also known as Sang, has had its numbers diminished greatly by collectors who sell the dried roots as a medicinal. The genus name *Panax* means "all-healing," and the plants are known worldwide as a tonic for practically any illness. Many unsubstantiated claims have been made, but there is some evidence that there may be some protection against stress effects. Powers of concentration and prevention of fatigue are also indicated by decreases in errors made in the performance of tasks.

Ginseng is a perennial herb that survives in scattered sites of rich woods mostly in the mountains.

Ginseng
Panax quinquefolius

Ginseng Family
Araliaceae

This little shrub would appear to qualify as an example of nature's custom-tailoring that assembles precisely a variety of parts to fit a specific need. It is a common plant of delicate beauty that forms spreading colonies, and it finds a home in the dry exposed soils of thin woods and roadsides, which also seem to be spreading. The plant group to which it belongs is one respected since ancient times for its ornamental qualities, and it is probably more plentiful and widespread than our other wild roses.

A low-growing species often not much branched, it is not usually more than 3 feet tall. The green to reddish stems are slender and are equipped with straight, needlelike prickles about a quarter-inch long.

The smooth, dark green leaves are composed of usually 5, occasionally 7, oval and toothed leaflets. Overall leaf size is about 3 or 4 inches.

The fragrant deep pink to red-pink flowers bloom from May to July. They are in clusters of 2 or 3 or are solitary and measure 2 to 2½ inches across.

Several tiny fruits develop within each flower from August to October and become enclosed by the enlarged floral base to form an orange red to red hip about a half-inch in diameter that persists through the winter.

Another species, *R. palustris,* is similar and abundant. Its leaves have 5 to 9, but more often 7, leaflets, and its prickles are down-curved.

Other names given to Carolina Rose are Pasture Rose, Low Rose, and Wild Rose. Its habitats are the rocky or sandy soils of open fields and wood borders, roadsides and thickets.

Roses are known for the most part by the elaborate products of horticulture; nevertheless somehow there is a certain directness in the beauty of the wild rose that is lost to the sophisticated flower of the garden.

Carolina Rose

Rosa carolina

Rose Family

Rosaceae

The group of plants known as hawthorns is a large one. They comprise many species that are very difficult to separate. They are very similar to one another, and they are highly variable. Despite the difficulty in identifying species, it is almost always easy to recognize a plant as being a member of the hawthorns.

Dwarf Hawthorn is one of the more easily identified members of the group. It is a shrub from 1 to 5 feet tall, whereas the other species are trees or much larger shrubs. The branches are very slender and tend to spread irregularly. The stems are hairy when young and bear a few to many slender, straight, and sharp thorns that are from 1 to 2 inches long.

The shiny, deep green leaves are small and oval with the widest portion often nearer the tip. There are blunt teeth and sometimes slight lobing along the margins, and the undersides are softly hairy.

The flowers open in May and are small and white with rounded petals. They are borne singly or with not more than 3 in a cluster.

The fruits that ripen during October resemble little apples. They are about one-half inch or a little less in diameter and vary in color from greenish or brownish yellow to red or orange. The lower portion of the flower usually persists on the fruit as 5 pointed and toothed leaflike structures.

There are three species, *C. crus-galli, C. punctata,* and *C. flava,* that have leaves similar to Dwarf Hawthorn, but all three have fruits about twice as large. The first mentioned has thorns 2 to 5 inches long that frequently themselves have thorns, and the second produces flowers in large clusters.

Dwarf Hawthorn, sometimes shortened to Dwarf Thorn, is a very attractive hardy ornamental plant that grows in sandy or rocky open woods or thickets. Hawthorns can be propagated by seed sown in the fall, and small plants are easily transplanted.

Dwarf Hawthorn

Crataegus uniflora

Rose Family

Rosaceae

A dense, matted growth of dark green foliage, red berries, and white flowers marks the borders of swamps and bogs where cranberries are found. The leafy mantle is durable year-round, since this is an evergreen species, and contrasting dots of red are visible for more than half the year due to the long-lasting fruits.

The slender stems trail along the ground branching frequently and proliferating numerous short erect branches clothed with rich, green, oblong leaves that often show a reddish cast in winter.

In June and July the graceful flowers that appear are remindful of shooting stars. The long, purplish red stamens protrude, the pink to white petals are backswept, and the flower nods from a very slender curving stalk.

The shining red fruits ripen from August to November as berries one-half to three-fourths of an inch in diameter, and these remain throughout the winter and into the spring.

The Southern Mountain Cranberry, *V. erythrocarpum*, is a deciduous species with much larger oval leaves and much smaller and darker berries that have little or no flavor. This plant too is found in bogs, but it also inhabits much drier sites such as moist woodlands.

The common name of the species is thought to have arisen from the fancied resemblance of the unopened flower buds on their slender, curved stalks to the head and neck of a crane.

Cranberry, also called American Cranberry and Large Cranberry, is the cranberry of commerce.

Growth requirements of the plant are those of the swamps and bogs, an acid environment with ever-present wet soil.

Cranberry

Heath Family

Vaccinium macrocarpon

Ericaceae

One of the times of outstanding floral beauty in the mountains is the peak of the flowering period of Mountain Laurel. The summer woodlands and rocky slopes are abundantly decked with the colorful pink blossoms that cluster at the stem tips of this attractive plant. However, the end of flowering is not final, for in the fall the leaves remain with their rich green, now contrasted with the red-purple assemblies of slenderly stalked fruits whose pincushion effect seems in keeping with the prickle of the autumn air.

An evergreen species usually shrubby and 3 to 10 feet tall, it sometimes attains a height of 20 to 30 feet. Its stout and often crooked branches diverge irregularly and frequently form dense thickets.

The lustrous dark green foliage consists of oval, pointed leaves 2 to 5 inches long with a smooth and leathery texture.

The rose-pink to white flowers appear from May until July. They are interesting in that their pressure-sensitive stamens facilitate pollination by closing quickly on visiting insects.

The fruits develop from August to October as small globular capsules a quarter-inch across that finally turn a light brown and split into five parts.

Another species, *K. angustifolia,* is rare and has narrow leaves in pairs or circles of 3 with flowers from the sides rather than the tips of the stems.

Mountain Laurel is also called Calico Bush, Ivy, and Spoonwood. It is as poisonous as it is attractive, as are many other members of the family. There are reports of honey being poisoned from bees visiting the flowers.

It is found in rocky or sandy woods or clearings. Its hardiness and beauty in foliage, flower, and fruit make it a highly desirable evergreen shrub.

It is propagated by seeds sown in the early spring and kept inside until the following season. They should not be planted in limestone or clay soils.

Mountain Laurel

Heath Family

Kalmia latifolia

Ericaceae

An extremely fortunate blend of remarkable beauty and common occurrence, Flowering Dogwood is in the judgment of many the most ornamental of our native trees. It is a familiar small tree usually of shrublike habit throughout the mountains, ordinarily at low to medium elevations. The widely spreading branches, often arising from multiple trunks, curve upward near their tips where the younger stems take on a greenish to purplish smoky gray cast.

The broadly oval leaves grow in pairs along the stem. Their blades have smooth margins that taper abruptly to a short point, and the conspicuous veins curve from the midrib toward the tip. In the autumn the leaves turn bright red.

The tiny greenish yellow flowers develop in small clusters during April and May before the leaves appear. Each cluster is centered within four large white or occasionally pink bracts that are often mistaken for the petals of a single flower.

In September and October the ripened fruits are represented by a cluster of deep scarlet berrylike ovoids with black beaks. These fruits are a source of food for birds, squirrels, and other species of wildlife.

Only one other species, *C. canadensis,* has red fruits. It is a more northern and much rarer plant that is also the only other that has a similar but smaller floral cluster; however, it is only 4 to 9 inches tall.

The wood of Flowering Dogwood is extremely hard and strong and has been used in making such things as tool handles and golf club heads. The young stems have been used as "chewing sticks" for the purpose of teeth cleaning and combating fever.

This plant is found in woodlands in all except very wet or very high elevations. It is probably more often cultivated as an ornamental than any other native tree.

Flowering Dogwood

Dogwood Family

Cornus florida

Cornaceae

Mountain Ash in the summer is a small rounded tree clothed in a thick blanket of large, bright green, and much-divided leaves that lend a fernlike effect. Scattered throughout the dense foliage and in contrast to the rich green are broad patches of white provided by the abundant clusters of flowers. Then in the autumn to the green of the foliage is added a suffusion of reddish bronze, and the once white floral patches now glisten with masses of bright red fruits.

The trunk is smooth and gray with slender branches that form a rounded crown that usually reaches a height of not more than 30 feet.

The leaves are 6 to 8 inches long and up to 4 inches wide. The blades are composed of many oblong pointed leaflets with toothed margins, and the stalks are a purplish red.

The small white flowers alone are inconspicuous, but the rounded to flattened clusters are dense and numerous and often measure 6 inches across. The flowering period comes in May and June.

The fruits ripen during September and October as lustrous orange-red to red globes on slender red stalks. These fruits are frequently described as berry-like, but a closer look reveals them to have a great similarity to miniature apples. Cutting of the fruit with a sharp blade shows their structure to be that of an apple.

A European introduction, *P. aucuparia,* is widely planted as an ornamental that sometimes escapes. Its leaves are hairy underneath, and its larger fruits are nearly a half-inch across.

Mountain Ash, also American Mountain Ash, Roundwood, and Dogberry, is found in mountain woods and shrub balds and is more common at higher elevations.

A very ornamental species in summer and fall, it grows better in cool moist mountains. It can be propagated by seeds sown in the fall.

Mountain Ash

Pyrus americana

Rose Family

Rosaceae

An unusual plant in several respects, the angular green stems branch widely and irregularly to form an open and very often oddly shaped yet attractive small shrub. The foliage consists of bright green leaves that have sharp points and are finely toothed along the margins.

During the flowering period of May and June slender stalks from near the base of the leaves bear curiously shaped and colored flowers. The petals are almost round, and there is a round disk located in the center, so that the flowers appear as an arrangement of circles. Pigmentation may be green, yellowish green, or greenish purple.

The flowers, though interesting in color and form, are small, and such a striking alteration in appearance takes place when fruits are ripened that floral status is forgotten. The fruits mature during September and October, whereby introduction of new shapes and hues eclipses all else. The fruit is usually formed of 4 or 5 lobes that are rough with wartlike projections. The color varies from deep pink to deep purplish red, and when the lobes separate to reveal the scarlet coat of the seeds, an unusual color combination results.

A somewhat similar but larger plant, *E. atropurpurens*, has dark purple or maroon flowers and smooth fruits.

It is not difficult to see how Strawberry Bush also was given the name Bursting Heart.

This plant is found in mixed deciduous woods that may vary from moist to very wet. Propagation is by seeds left exposed to winter temperatures. The species is tolerant to a wide range of soil types.

Strawberry Bush

Euonymus americanus

Staff-tree Family

Celastraceae

The soils of low-lying wetlands generally support a population of this large deciduous shrub which contributes to the vegetational cover a profusion of spreading, gray-barked branches clothed in rich, dark green foliage. In the spring and early summer the verdure is dotted with many tiny white flowers that are rather inconspicuous, but autumn brings a change that establishes Winterberry as one of our highly ornamental native shrubs. Fruiting is almost always heavy, and the stems are thickly clustered, many of them hidden, by the bright red berrylike fruits that remain on the branches relatively unchanged after all the leaves have fallen and far on into the winter.

The stems branch widely and attain a height of 4 to 20 feet. The foliage is variable but consists usually of leaves about 1 to 4 inches long that taper abruptly to a point. Their blades are toothed or notched along the margins and conspicuously wrinkled with heavy veining.

The flowering period during May and June produces the tiny white flowers closely along the stems, singly or in very small clusters.

The fruits develop and mature from September to November as densely clustered bright red balls approximately one-quarter inch in diameter.

The evergreen and spiny-toothed leaves of American Holly, *I. opaca,* easily identify it, but there is another species, *I. montana,* that is much more similar to Winterberry. Its leaves are 2 to 7 inches long, usually gradually tapered to a long point, and less conspicuously wrinkled.

Winterberry is also known as Black Alder, since its leaves blacken in the autumn, and it inhabits about the same areas as Alder. Both are found in low woods, swamps, wet thickets, and stream and pond margins.

The handsome foliage and colorful, long-lasting fruits make Winterberry a good choice for ornamental planting in wet areas.

Winterberry

Ilex verticillata

Holly Family

Aquifoliaceae

In the autumn of the year and on into the winter fencerows are sometimes ornamented with splashes of orange and red when the fruits and seeds of this woody vine mature.

The stems climb upon fences, shrubs, and trees by twining, or they may produce a sprawling pattern of growth by straggling along the ground and over low vegetation. The dark green leaves are oblong and pointed with very small teeth along the margins.

During May and June elongate clusters of small, greenish white or greenish yellow flowers grow from the ends of the stems. The size and color of the inflorescence do not make for a conspicuous display, but this is more than compensated by the form and color of the rich green foliage and especially by the striking hues of the fruiting condition.

The clusters of orange or yellowish orange fruits take on an additional color as the fruit walls separate to reveal the crimson seeds within. These colorful fruiting clusters are long-lasting and are frequently collected for decorative purposes. The plant grows well in a variety of habitats and is sometimes cultivated.

Another very similar species is *C. orbiculatus,* an introduction from Asia, that is planted as an ornamental but occasionally escapes into the wild. There are usually only 3 or fewer flowers in a cluster that arises from the angle between the leaf and stem, and the leaves are often almost circular in outline.

Bittersweet is also called American Bittersweet, Climbing Bittersweet, and Waxwort. This plant is found in woods, wood borders, thickets, and occasionally on roadside banks.

Bittersweet

Celastrus scandens

Celastraceae

This plant produces no flowers, fruits, or seeds, nor is there even a stem that is visible. The stem, or rhizome, is underground, so the only parts of the plant that are ordinarily seen are the leaves and the spore cases they produce. In many species of ferns, however, the characteristics of the foliage and the structures involved in the formation of spores are quite attractive and often lend a distinctive mien to the tracts of land in which they grow.

The leaves or fronds of Royal Fern grow in dense clusters and often attain a height of 6 feet with a blade width that may be nearly 2 feet. These palmlike fronds are divided into 5 to 7 pairs of large segments which are then divided again into many elongated segments that are tapered to a blunt point.

From May through July spore cases will form on some of the fronds while others are sterile. The site of spore-case formation of the fertile fronds is at the apex of the blade. Several of the uppermost large segments of the frond are highly reduced in size, and it is on these reduced segments that great numbers of minute rounded and pear-shaped spore cases are formed. They develop in many slender clusters which in maturing take on a rich brown color.

Two other species in the genus are common. Interrupted Fern, *O. claytoniana,* forms darker spore cases on several middle segments of the fronds. Cinnamon Fern, *O. cinnamomea,* is a shorter plant with separate fertile fronds wherein all leaf segments form yellowish brown spore clusters.

Royal Fern has also acquired the names King Fern, and Flowering Fern. It is a highly ornamental species suitable for open sunny and moist areas. The large clumps develop extensive roots requiring a good depth of soil.

Its habitats are moist woods, swamps, marshes, and streamsides. Propagation can be carried out by planting cuttings of the underground stems.

Royal Fern

Osmunda regalis

Passersby are likely to have their attention attracted to Sweet Cicely by the handsome foliage or the clusters of white flowers; however, the breaking of a stem may cause one to be aware of this plant even before it is seen. The broken stem releases an aromatic fragrance closely resembling that of licorice or anise, and the roots are even more strongly scented.

This is a perennial herb that grows from a much thickened root to a height of 1 foot to over 3 feet. The stems are rather stout and smooth and often widely branched.

The leaves are relatively large, their blades being divided into several small leaflets usually in groups of 3. Each leaflet is toothed along the margin and tapered gradually to a point.

The very small flowers that open in April and May form small clusters at the ends of long stalks. Termination of flowering is followed by the formation of interestingly structured fruits that are green from late May through June.

The fruits mature from July to October, and the ripening brings a change in color from green to black. The shape is slender and pointed at both ends remindful of a tiny cigar. There are minute bristles on the surface and twin pointed projections at the tip.

One other species, *O. claytoni,* is almost identical but has barely visible points at the fruit tip and usually hairy stems.

Sweet Cicely also answers to the names Smooth Sweet Cicely, Anise Root, and Sweet Chervil.

Moist woods and stream banks are habitats of this species. It can be grown from seed planted in autumn, and it does well and adds to the appearance of a partially shaded site.

Sweet Cicely

Osmorhiza longistylis

Parsley Family

Umbelliferae

On seeing this plant in late summer one's first impression is that somehow a crop of blackberries or raspberries has developed up among the shining green leaves of a spreading bushy tree. It is at this time, when the fruits are in the midst of their display of color transition, that the most attractive features of the species are seen in combination.

This is a small tree usually less than 40 feet tall with a rounded crown and sometimes the stature of a large shrub. The smooth, bright green leaves are glossy, have toothed margins, and offer considerable variety in form. Heart-shaped leaves may predominate, or mixtures of oblong to nearly round may be observed, but usually there are variously lobed specimens.

The flowers are minute and appear in very short strings in May and June. These slender flowering clusters are inconspicuous, but the fruits that are produced from June to August are quite colorful. The mulberries change from green to white, pink, purple, or black and are edible and sweet.

Another mulberry, *M. rubra,* has similar edible fruits, but the leaves are dull green and rough above while hairy underneath.

White Mulberry is a native of China and has long been in cultivation primarily for its leaves as a food for the silkworm. After introduction into this country, it was frequently planted as an ornamental and for the fruits, which are also eaten by birds and other wildlife species. It has escaped into many areas of the eastern part of the country.

It is established in open woods, pastures, fields, and roadsides. The plant can be grown from seed and does well in almost any kind of soil.

White Mulberry

Mulberry Family

Morus alba

Moraceae

Several hairy stems diverge from the base and branch freely to produce a bushy plant one-half foot to more than 2-feet tall.

The leaves are hairy and have long stalks. The blades are divided usually into 5 to 7 oblong lobes that are in turn cleft into several narrow lobes.

The flowers come in from May to July arranged in loose clusters in the angle between stem and leaf stalk or in dense clusters at the stem ends. The petal color varies from pink to very pale pink or white with pink lines.

The thickly branched and spreading pattern of stems with their display of the fingerlike lobing of the leaves makes an attractive picture, but the flowers are pale, and it is during the fruiting period from June to August when more color and an interesting structure are added to the scene.

A slender, hairy cone is formed with the seeds at its base, encircled by the remaining lower portion of the flower. The whole structure changes from green to brown, but then all or some parts of the old floral base and the cone take on various shades of red. When the seeds are released, five threadlike tails curl from the cone and detach.

The geraniums are generally similar, but *G. maculatum* is larger overall and has purplish flowers. *G. columbinum* and *G. molle* have purplish flowers; the former has long flower stalks, while the latter is very softly hairy.

Carolina Cranesbill inhabits dry woods, roadsides, pastures, fields, and vacant lots. It can be grown from seed and does well in almost any soil.

Carolina Cranesbill

Geranium carolinianum

Geranium Family

Geraniaceae

This small perennial herb is 8 to 18 inches tall and appears to have a straight, slender stem that bears many leaves. In reality the extremely small stem is barely visible above ground, and there is usually only a single leaf divided into many parts. A separate and shorter stalk bears the flowers and fruits.

The tall leaf stalk is divided into 3 branches, each of which produces 3 to 5 oval leaflets that are pointed and finely toothed.

From May to June the tiny greenish white flowers appear. The flowering stalk develops from 2 to 7, commonly 3 branches, each with a rounded, many-flowered cluster at the tip. This flowering arrangement is positioned beneath the leaflets.

The fruiting process that occurs from June to August forms handsome spheres of glossy deep purple to black berrylike fruits that have minute 5-parted beaks.

There are 3 other much larger species with similar foliage, flower, and fruit structures. *A. racemosa* and *A. hispida* are herbs. The former can be 10 feet tall with yard-long leaves, while the latter is about 3 feet tall with thorny stems. *A. spinosa* is a large shrub with prickdly stems and leaves and huge flowering and fruiting clusters.

Small Spikenard is another name for Wild Sarsaparilla, as is False Sang, for its fancied resemblance to Ginseng, or Sang, another member of the family. Ginseng roots are used for medicinal purposes, and Wild Sarsaparilla's aromatic roots were used by the American Indians to make cough syrup and have been used as a substitute for the flavoring sarsaparilla which comes commercially from a tropical species of *Smilax* or Greenbrier.

It is a woodland plant that can be grown from seeds planted in rich soil.

Wild Sarsaparilla

Aralia nudicaulis

Ginseng Family

Araliaceae

Coming upon a colony of these plants may arouse memories of paintings depicting some artist's conception of our planet at an earlier age. There is the feeling of being in the presence of an ancient life form somehow transported to modern times. As a matter of fact, this species is a member of a group that indeed traces back to the remote past wherein it formed a much larger part of the flora of the Earth.

The straight, dark green stems are evergreen and stand 2 to 4 feet tall. There are usually no branches, and the surface bears many ridges and furrows. The tissues have a rough texture from the content of silica deposited by the cells.

The leaves are highly reduced in size and fused into a series of sheaths along the stem. The tips of the leaves often drop from the plant, leaving a black band encircling the stem. The sheaths frequently whiten as they age.

These plants do not produce flowers, fruits, or seeds. Their spores are formed in clusters of spore cases that appear as black, conelike structures at the apex of the stem.

There is a smaller species, *E. arvense,* that has separate fertile and sterile stems. The fertile stems are pinkish and unbranched, while the sterile ones are green and profusely branched.

Scouring Rush has been put to use as a light sandpaper taking advantage of the natural deposition of silica in the stem tissues. This abrasive quality still calls the species into use by campers in cleaning pots and pans.

This plant grows along roadsides and stream banks and in moist woods frequently in sandy soil. The spores and underground stems can be planted in moist soil and will grow in rather dense colonies. Planting in areas used by grazing animals is risky, since poisoning has been known to occur.

Scouring Rush

Equisetum hyemale

Horsetail Family

Equisetaceae

Handling almost any part of Velvet Leaf gives rise to the thought that a name comparing the entire plant to velvet could have been just as easily, and far more fittingly, applied. Practically every surface is densely covered with fine soft hairs that simulate the feel of the fabric velvet.

The thick, smooth stems are branched and may attain a height of 5 to 6 feet. The stems bear large leaves that have long stalks and heart-shaped blades that taper to a slender point. They are frequently about as wide as they are long, and the margins have small, sometimes indistinct, teeth.

Flowering takes place from July to September and produces yellow to orange-yellow flowers an inch or less in diameter. These flowers are fairly showy, but the structures that come into existence after the flowers fall are the ones most often remembered as the trademark of the species.

From each flower the fruit develops as a crown of radiating hornlike projections that form a corrugated surface. This configuration was put to use as an instrument for imprinting designs, and as a consequence the species acquired the functional names Stamp Weed, Pie Marker, and Butter Print.

The attractiveness of the colorful flowers, ample foliage, and unique fruit architecture caused the plant to be brought into this country for ornamental planting, and the country to which the species is indigenous supplied yet another name, Indian Mallow, referring not to the American Indian but to India.

This plant is an annual herbaceous species that grows up, produces flowers, and matures fruit very rapidly. It has escaped to open fields, roadsides, vacant lots, and cultivated land.

Propagation is by seed, and as indicated by the cited habitats the seeds germinate and growth occurs in very rich and very poor soils in open areas.

Velvet Leaf

Abutilon theophrasti

Mallow Family

Malvaceae

The mention of Cattail brings to mind areas of wet or muddy ground or standing water. This plant that is so naturally associated with watery sites may not be so readily associated with wildflowers by many people. The bright colors and recognizable parts of the familiar flower are not there.

The straight, stout stems, sheathed at their bases by the long, narrow leaves, stand 3 to 10 feet tall with the rich brown and velvety "cat's tail" at the tip.

The leaves are usually taller than the stem and are up to an inch in width. The leaf blades are flat and enclose the stem at the base.

The typical floral structures are not exhibited in this species, because the flowers are minute and appear to be a tiny cluster of bristles. There are thousands of these flowers crowded together into a cylindrical mass 2 to 8 inches long and one half to an inch and a half thick. These flowers are all female and make up the "cat's tail." The male flowers form a similar but more slender structure adjacent to and above the females. The male flowers fall from the plant shortly after pollen is released, and only a shriveling stalk remains.

Flowering occurs from May to July, and the fruits develop and ripen from June through November. The tiny fruits are seedlike and inconspicuous, but each produces a tuft of soft hairs that form a fluffy, cloudlike mass when the great number of tightly packed fruits separate and break up the "cat's tail."

Other names for this species are Common Cattail, Broadleaved Cattail, and Reed Mace.

It is found on stream and pond margins and in shallow water and wet ditches. The plant can be propagated from the underground stems, which will produce colonies in almost any sites with very wet soil.

Cattail

Typha latifolia

The narrow, oblong crown of this irregularly branching deciduous tree usually stands 30 to 60 feet tall but sometimes reaches 100 feet. The older bark of the often crooked trunks is dark brown and scaly, but that of the younger branches is extremely smooth and green or a rich copper color marked with conspicuous horizontal lines. In the spring the flowers appear and shower the shining green foliage with a multitude of white, fingerlike clusters. In late summer and autumn these clusters are converted to mixtures of red, purple, and black ripening cherries.

The leaves are 2 to 5 inches long with blades that are glossy above and margins beset with incurved teeth.

The very small white flowers bloom in May and are arranged in dense, cylindrical clusters 3 to 6 inches long and 1 to 2 inches thick.

The small cherries that mature in August and September are about one-half inch in diameter and very deep purple or black when fully ripe. These lustrous fruits are tartly sweet and edible. They are favorites of many birds.

A shrubby cherry, *P. virginiana,* is similar in leaf, flower, and fruit to Black Cherry bur differs in having shorter leaves with straight, sharp teeth, shorter and thicker flower clusters, and red fruits.

Black Cherry, also called Wild Cherry, Wild Black Cherry, and Rum Cherry, has had extracts of its bark used as an ingredient of tonics and cold remedies, but its leaves are poisonous to livestock and humans. The wood is a choice item in cabinetmaking.

This species is found in woods and fields and along fencerows and roadsides. It is a tree attractive in bark tones with handsome foliage, a pleasing spring floral display, and colorful fruits that attract birdlife. Exposed or partly shaded sites are suitable, and propagation is easily done with seed planting.

Black Cherry

Prunus serotina

Rose Family

Rosaceae

To those familiar with our southeastern seacoast, the appearance of this plant may engender a feeling that either the plant or the observer is out of place, for it is likely to recall the colonies of Sea Oats that fringe the sand dunes along the beaches from Virginia southward. Wild Oats is a similar but smaller and more delicate species of the same genus.

It is a perennial grass with spreading rhizomes that send up 3- to 4-foot slender and pliant stems that form thick colonies.

The long, narrow leaf blades taper gradually to a point and extend from sheaths that encircle the stems. They are bright green and often 8 inches in length.

The flowering and fruiting period extends through the summer and into the fall. In many of the grass species neither the flowers nor the fruits themselves ordinarily provide much of a conspicuous display. They are both very small and contained within scalelike structures making them essentially invisible. In this species, however, the broad and pointed enclosing scales overlap to form flattened ovals a half-inch to nearly 2 inches long. At first green many of them undergo a color change, and during late September and October they hang as light brown disks nodding in open graceful clusters from their slender, flexible stalks.

A less common species, *U. laxa,* is a smaller plant with very small flowering and fruiting structures arranged in stiffly erect clusters.

Wild Oats is also known as Spike Grass, and it is found in moist woods, thickets, and ditches.

An attractive grass, it is a good soil holder that will grow well in moist, shady locations. The tall, slender stems, flexuous inflorescences, and colonial habit make an ornamental combination. The rhizomes can be divided and planted.

Wild Oats

Uniola latifolia

Grass Family

Gramineae

The importance of grasses to man as a food source is unarguable, and many have long been staples in the field of landscaping. Their flowers and fruits, however, are usually reduced in size and subdued in color with the result that they are sometimes slighted as wildflowers. The graceful, curving, bristly arcs of the "foxtails" of this plant wave from the tips of straight, slender, and smooth stems that often reach a height of 5 or 6 feet.

The long narrow blades of the leaves are pointed, about half an inch wide, as much as 8 inches long and invested with very small hairs.

From July until October the flowers and fruits are formed. Minute flowers are concealed within a series of small scales arranged in elongate, flexible, and bristly clusters 3 to 6 inches long. When the fruits have developed the weight of the crowded oval grains accentuates the curve of the stalk.

There are three other species that are very similar to this one. The most similar is *S. viridis,* which has shorter flowering and fruiting clusters that are usually stiffly erect. The leaves of *S. glauca* are whitish and tend to be twisted or spiraled, while its bristles are yellowish. The stems of *S. geniculata* are often bent near the base, and the bristles are usually purplish.

Foxtail is also known by the names Foxtail Grass, Bristlegrass, and Bristly Foxtail.

This grass came into this country from China and has established itself and spread quickly in the disturbed soils of roadsides, fields, and cultivated land.

Weedy grasses are not ordinarily thought of as decorative, yet the tufts of tall, straight stems with their curving clusters of bristles has a pleasing effect. This annual species grows very well in poor dry soils of exposed sites and is easily propagated by seeds.

Foxtail

Setaria faberii

Grass Family

Gramineae

Spanish Needles in all likelihood needs no introduction to anyone. Despite the fact that it is one of the most common weeds in almost any kind of soil in the eastern half of the country, it is one of the very easiest species to become attached to. Those who venture into the woods and fields in the autumn can be assured that they stand to gain something from their association with this plant.

The slender, branching stems of this annual herb are square and smooth. The height of the plant ranges from less than a foot to about 5 feet.

The leaves occur in pairs and have long slender stalks. The blades are divided into several deeply cut segments that are again deeply or shallowly divided into more or less rounded lobes.

The flowers open during late July and August. The flowers are highly reduced in size and are tightly packed in small clusters, sometimes fairly bright yellow but often dull yellowish green.

The fruits mature from August through October as slender, needlelike objects a half-inch to an inch long. At the tips of these "needles" are 3 or 4 sharply barbed bristles. As the fruit clusters ripen, they diverge to form a starlike arrangement whose profile is another of autumn's symbols, and whose barbs now are presented in every direction to make the acquaintance of passersby.

There are several species in the genus, but the fruits of the others are all flattened and shorter. When ripe, all these fruits readily detach, and the barbs stick tightly to almost any fabric or pelt, an effective means of seed dissemination. The group as a whole is referred to by the name Beggar Ticks.

Spanish Needles inhabits roadsides, fields, pastures, and open woods.

Spanish Needles

Composite Family

Bidens bipinnata

Compositae

Jimson Weed is a plant of contradictions. It seems that listing its features brings up about as many undesirable ones as desirable ones.

It has a large attractive flower whose white or violet petals form a flared tube somewhat resembling a trumpet, but the flowers have an unpleasant odor.

The fruits are spiny ovals with collarlike remnants of the flowers encircling their bases. These fruits possess a structural grace, but there is the counterbalancing fact that the contained seeds are deadly poison.

Even the origin of the species presents a problem. There are literature citations to the effect that the plant was introduced into the United States from Asia, but there are also references to the tragic consequences befalling those who had eaten it by the early settlers in Virginia. As a matter of fact, the name Jimson Weed is an alteration of Jamestown Weed.

The smooth, stout stems may be green, green tinged with purple, or purple. They follow a pattern of wide-branching growth to a height of as much as 6 feet.

The leaves are very thin and pointed with margins of large, irregular teeth that lend a ragged appearance. Leaves that have been bruised are ill-scented.

The flowers are about 4 inches long, having the open end flared into pointed lobes and the closed end covered by a green angular sleeve.

The fruit is a spiny dome with a saucerlike or collarlike shelf at its base. The black seed within, as cited, can be lethal, but all parts of this plant are poisonous. Yet stramonium comes from this species and has the same medical use as belladonna, another useful drug from a different member of this family.

The form of the fruit has given the plant the name Thorn Apple.

Pastures, fields, and roadsides are the usual habitats.

Jimson Weed

Datura stramonium

Nightshade Family

Solanaceae

When one visualizes the picturesque scenery of a creek or pond, one image that nearly always comes to mind is the familiar blending of the water's edge with the alders. Many streams are shaded and cooled in summer under the thickets and natural hedges formed by the numerous spreading branches of these tall and leafy shrubs.

The height in this species ranges from 6 to 15 feet, and often the plants are as wide as they are tall. The stems bear an abundance of dark green leaves that are oblong with rounded or blunt-pointed tips and are often wider near the tip. The veining pattern of the blade is distinctly parallel, and the margins are finely toothed.

The flowers and fruits are minute and are housed within a series of small flattened and overlapping scales. Flowering occurs in March, and the scales enclosing the male flowers develop into a slender, yellowish brown, taillike structure that hangs from the stem. The tiny fruits are flattened and rounded to squarish nuts that mature from August to October within a woody cone that sits upright on the stem. The cone is reddish to purplish brown and remains conspicuous on the plant all during autumn and winter.

Another much less common species, *A. rugosa,* is quite similar to this one, but the underside of the leaf is a much paler green, or it is whitened, and the stems are speckled. Some lump the two together as a single species.

Common Alder is also known as Smooth Alder, Hazel Alder, and Brookside Alder. A bark extract was used by the American Indians for treatment of burns and indigestion. The pollen has been cited as allergenic.

It is found in wet woods, marshes, streamsides, and pond edges. It can be propagated by seed sown in the spring or by cuttings.

Common Alder

Alnus serrulata

Hazel Family

Corylaceae

Those who frequent the outdoors are familiar with Cocklebur as a plant that is at times no more than a minor nuisance but again is capable of making what might be called a lasting impression. At the bases of the upper leaves there are dense clusters of oval prickly burs that are very easily dislodged by slight contact, whereupon they adhere tightly to almost any kind of clothing that may be readily penetrated by some of the sharp, rigid spines.

The tiny flowers are inconspicuous or absent by the time fruiting occurs in October and November, and the leaves are showing the effects of wear and tear. Yet despite the lack of floral color, a prickly and weedy reputation, and a somewhat bedraggled appearance, there is still a singular beauty in the mixture of jagged leaves and the tangle of green and brown burrs that seems to be emblematic of the ending of autumn and the beginning of winter.

This plant is usually 1 foot to 5 feet tall with large, long-stalked leaves whose triangular blades are about as broad as long and are irregularly toothed and lobed.

The minute male and female flowers grow in separate clusters, and pairs of the females are enclosed within a hard, bristly sheath that later becomes the burr within which will develop two flattened oblong fruits. The burrs are covered with spines having hooked tips, and at the end are two longer straighter spines.

Cocklebur and another species, X. *spinosum.,* which has smaller slender leaves with a 3-pronged spine at their base, have pollen that is highly allergenic.

These annual herbs are also called Clobur and Burweed and are found in fields, along roadsides, in pastures, and in cultivated land.

Cocklebur

Xanthium strumarium

Composite Family

Compositae

This deciduous tree is usually 60 to 70 feet tall but may be much taller. The dark gray to brown bark may be thornless, or it may be covered with masses of thorns. These thorns may be simple and straight, or they may be compound and branched many times with a total length of 10 to 12 inches. The smaller branches and branchlets may be thorny throughout.

The leaves are large but are divided into many small leaflets that are often divided again into still smaller segments. Both kinds of subdivision of the leaves may be found on the same tree and on the same leaf.

The flowers are minute and inconspicuous, blooming in May and June and developing in greenish white strings. The fruits that follow when these flowers are pollinated and fertilized, however, constitute one of the major attractions of the plant.

The fruits ripen from July to November and hang in clusters of long, flat pods that are usually curved and often twisted. They are 5 to 15 inches long and 1 to 2 inches broad. The ripening process changes their color from green to brown, rust, or maroon. The seeds, whose position within the pod is visible externally, are implanted in a greenish yellow pulp that is sweet and edible.

Honey Locust, also known by the names Sweet Locust and Honey Shuck, is very much an ornamental species by way of its large and colorful fruits and the finely divided foliage that produces the effect of a green, lacelike mist. The formidable thorniness has a beauty of its own, but it can also present problems. There is, however, a form of the tree that is completely free of thorns.

This tree inhabits rich moist woods but will grow in almost any kind of soil. It is very hardy and can be propagated by seeds. Planting should be done in the spring, and some report better results after hot-water soaking.

Honey Locust

Gleditsia triacanthos

Pulse Family

Leguminosae

Princess Tree is quite a striking specimen at the beginning of the growing season in early spring. It is one of those trees with large and colorful flowers that appear before the leaves have expanded. The stout, spreading branches form a small to medium-sized deciduous tree having a width that many times equals or exceeds its height.

The large, heart-shaped leaves grow in pairs and are frequently 12 inches long and almost as wide. They unfold immediately after the flowers develop and are one of the prominent features of the species.

The flaring, trumpetlike flowers are pale purple and measure 2 or 3 inches in length. They open in April and May and hang in large clusters, usually in great quantity. The leaves are not fully expanded at this time, making the flowers highly visible, and this, coupled with the large floral size and color, make for an especially handsome display.

The fruits that are produced are oval, pointed capsules an inch and a half or more in length. They mature during September and October and remain on the tree in large and numerous brown bunches throughout the winter along with the velvety tan or light brown buds of next season's flowers.

Without flowers or fruits, Princess Tree is sometimes confused with the Cigar Tree, *Catalpa speciosa,* since the leaves of these species are very similar; however, the leaves of the former occur most often in pairs, while those of the latter are usually in circles of three.

Princess Tree, a native of China, is also called Empress Tree, Imperial Tree, Royal Paulownia, and Karri Tree.

It has escaped from cultivation as an ornamental and has established itself along roadsides, in fencerows, and on wooded slopes. Propagation is by seeds sown in the spring and by root, stem, or very young leaf cuttings.

Princess Tree

Paulownia tomentosa

Figwort Family

Scrophulariaceae

An elegant little herb named in commemoration of the sorceress Medea, it has not thus far revealed any of the magical powers of healing or destruction possessed by its namesake; nonetheless, it is singular and enchanting in all particulars.

A white thickened and edible underground rhizome having a shape, texture, odor, and flavor resembling cucumber sends up straight and slender stems to a height of 1 to 3 feet. These stems are somewhat whitened with scattered tufts of soft woolly hairs and encircled near the midpoint by about a half-dozen large, pointed leaves and again at the summit by usually 3 smaller ones.

At the time of flowering in May and June, a small, few-flowered cluster appears at the tip of the stem. The flowers are not large, and they develop on stalks that curve downward, bringing them to a position beneath the upper circle of leaves. A cursory observation might not warrant a second look, which would reveal reflexed yellow sepals and petals crested with purple ascending stamens and surpassed by spreading recurved stigmas of purple to rust hues.

The products of fruiting, like those of flowering, underscore the peculiar beauty of Medea's memorial. In September and October the bases of the upper circle of leaves are blazed with red, and the drooping stalks that bore the flowers straighten to an erect position. At their tips materialize dark purple to ebony berries of a most exquisite luster.

The stems and leaves of an orchid, *Isotria verticillata,* are somewhat similar, but neither flowers nor fruits are at all alike.

Indian Cucumber-root also has the name Cushat Lily. It is a common species throughout moist rich woods and in the vicinity of bogs.

This is an attractive perennial herbaceous plant with interesting floral structure, foliage, and especially fruit; it can be grown easily from seeds.

Indian Cucumber-root

Medeola virginiana

Lily Family

Liliaceae

In the early summer the deep green of the foliage is broken here and there by flashes of white as the wind exposes the undersides of the leaves, and long, slender stalks of yellowish green to yellow flowers wave from the widely spreading reddish brown branches. By autumn the stems are hung with clusters of the yellowish green and spiny burrs that are products of the fruiting process. In the last phase of ripening these burrs open to reveal the lustrous dark brown to nearly black nuts.

Chinquapin is usually a shrub about 4 to 15 feet high, yet it does develop into a bushy tree more than 20 feet tall. The stems are thickly branched and wide-spreading.

The oblong leaves are 2 to 8 inches long with toothed margins and pointed or rounded tips. The undersides are covered with a dense growth of white hairs.

The very small, yellowish flowers grow in slenderly elongate clusters 2 to 6 inches long. The flowering period comes in June, and the plant is usually thickly populated with the conspicuous tassels.

The fruiting burr is sharply spiny and an inch or more across. It contains a single sweet and edible nut one-half to three-quarters of an inch long.

Chestnut, *C. dentata,* is similar in leaf and fruit, but the leaves are longer and green beneath, and the larger burrs contain 2 or 3 nuts.

The fruits of Chinquapin, also called Dwarf Chestnut, are smaller than Chestnut but are very palatable to man and many species of wildlife.

Dry woods and thickets, habitats of this species, make it an excellent choice for planting in partially shaded and dry sites. Its attractive foliage and thick growth make a good hedge with a handsome display of flowers, and the edible fruits are a bonus.

Chinquapin

Castanea pumila

Beech Family

Fagaceae

The theme of this species is prickliness. The rough, prickly stems oftentimes reach a height of almost 10 feet, and at their tops sit the large and equally prickly flowering heads of the summer months and the fruiting heads of autumn, which persist throughout the winter.

The paired leaves are prickly along their margins and along the midrib beneath. Leaf size is large in general but especially at the base of the plant where it may measure well over a foot. Some of the upper leaf pairs are joined at their bases, thus encircling and forming a pocket around the stem.

From July to September a large number of small pink, purple, or white flowers develop in a dense band around the middle of the cylindrical or egg-shaped head. Long, slender, and sharp spines protrude from between the flowers; and, curiously the floral band widens as flowers develop in both directions.

The very small fruits that mature during September and October are hardly visible on the spiny head; therefore, except for the loss of flower color, there is little change in appearance from the flowering condition.

Teasel is an introduced species from Europe, and there is another very similar species, *D. fullonum,* also European, that has not become established here but does have an interesting history of having been used to raise a nap on woolen fabric. The spines of the dried heads teased the cloth efficiently and caused less damage than the machinery then available.

The enduring quality of these spiny heads with the appearance of pincushions framed by gracefully arching spikes makes them excellent material for dried arrangements. The plant is best collected from its natural habitat than planted.

This biennial herb produces lush foliage the first year and the tall flowering stems the second; it grows along roadsides and fencerows and in pastureland.

Teasel

Dipsacus sylvestris

Autumn finds the leaves of this tall shrub still green and its slender branches bending under the burden of an immense crop of fruit. The dense, hanging clusters of small black to bluish black spheres grow in crowded masses throughout the plant and often persist through the winter.

The hairy, flexible stems undergo frequent branching that establishes a spreading pattern of growth. A height of from 4 to 10 feet is common for the species, but occasionally there are plants that reach 25 to 30 feet.

The leaves are borne in pairs and are oblong with both ends more or less rounded. They are semievergreen, remaining on the plant and retaining their dark green color during the fall months and often into the winter.

There is striking floral profusion that occurs during May and June when at the ends of almost all the stems are displayed loosely branching clusters of white flowers. The flowers are small, but the clusters are large and present in such great quantity that the entire complexion of the plant is significantly changed.

Several species of privet have been introduced into this country from Europe and Asia. They are all very similar, and some have escaped from cultivation in greater or lesser degrees. This species has established itself much better than the others in this area, and it can be distinguished from them by its flowers, which are less than one-quarter-inch long and its leaf stalks and young branches, which are both densely hairy.

Chinese Privet, a native of China and Korea, has become a part of the flora of open woods, fields, and roadsides. It is extensively cultivated for use as a hedge and is considered by many to be the handsomest of the privets.

Propagation is by seeds sown in the fall or by cuttings.

Chinese Privet

Olive Family

Ligustrum sinense

Oleaceae

This low herb usually stands less than a foot tall. The stems have a velvety texture due to a dense growth of minute soft hairs. The plant is generally well branched, often from ground level to the topmost portion of the main stem.

The stems are leafy almost throughout, and the larger basal leaves are wider and rounded at their tips. The leaves higher on the stem are shaped like arrowheads with a pair of lobes at the base extending one on either side of the stem.

Tiny white or greenish white flowers grow in very small inconspicuous clusters at the tips of the stems. The color and structure associated with fruit development provide the features that ordinarily attract attention to this species.

The fruits ripen on lengthening stalks and produce elongated arrangements of oval, flattened pods that are remindful of spoons or spades. These pods go through color changes from pale green to reddish purple or reddish brown to light or dark brown as they age. They mature in June and July and remain intact into the autumn.

There is another species similar to this one and found in the same habitats called Poor Man's Pepper, *L. virginicum*. It differs in its upper stem leaves, which are merely narrowed at the base without any basal lobes that lend the arrowhead effect.

Cow Cress is also called by the names Field Cress and Field Peppergrass. It is a weedy herbaceous annual plant that was introduced into this country from Europe; it has established itself widely in roadsides, old fields, pastures, and cultivated land.

Cow Cress

Lepidium campestre

Mustard Family

Cruciferae

The surfaces of springs and quiet flowing streams of cool water are sometimes dotted with the lush green cushions formed by the thickly matted and leafy stems of this aquatic herb.

The blades of the leaves are composed of several segments that are oval to nearly round, and the segment at the tip is generally larger and more rounded.

The flowers are formed from April until autumn. The arrangement of the 4 petals of each flower forms a small white cross. The small size of the flowers is offset by their development in numerous rounded clusters that are quite conspicuous against the dense foliage.

The fruiting process commences not long after flowering begins and continues on through October. As the fruits develop, the stalk bearing them lengthens, and an erect elongated cluster results. The fruits are slender, rounded pods that are curved and have a tiny, stemlike projection at the tip. As the seeds within the pods ripen, the color of the seeds and the walls of the pods are changed to a reddish brown, red, or purple.

Watercress was introduced into this country from Europe and has become naturalized throughout. The plant is both nutritious and palatable, having a high content of vitamins and proteins as well as the peppery taste that is characteristic of most of the mustards. It is collected for addition to salads for this pungent quality.

This perennial herbaceous species has established itself in many clear and uncontaminated streams and springs mostly in the mountains. It can be propagated by transference to such a habitat, but it is usually collected for use as a salad from the wild condition.

Watercress

Nasturtium officinale

Mustard Family

Cruciferae

Many plants possess more than one aesthetically appealing quality, but this one exhibits a procession of beauty beginning in the early spring and culminating during the autumn with its most colorful phases on display.

This deciduous tree may be small and shrublike or may attain a height of over 100 feet, and the entire plant is aromatic. Young stems are green or yellowish green and often have a white or bluish white coating that lends a frosted appearance.

The yellow to greenish yellow flower clusters are present before the leaves develop fully, so the floral show is highly visible. The flowers are either male or female, and each is found on a separate tree.

In April and May, with flowers already present, the leaves begin to enlarge and reveal a variety of shapes. There are leaves that look like mittens and some that resemble tridents, while others are ovals. This diversity of form combined with a deep green color makes this foliage unusually attractive, and the fall of the year brings a conversion to brilliant orange, yellow, and red.

Fruiting takes place from June to August on those trees bearing female flowers. The fruits are spherical and develop from green to blue or blue-black, while their stalks change to a bright red and become enlarged just beneath the fruits.

The spicy twigs are chewed as teeth cleaners, a tea is prepared from the bark of the roots, and other dental and medical remedies have been concocted from sassafras extracts; however, a component of sassafras oil has been cited as a carcinogen.

Sassafras grows in woods, roadsides, and fields and is described as a weed tree. It can be propagated by seed or by planting shoots that come off from or near the roots.

Sassafras

Sassafras albidum

Laural Family

Lauraceae

The blueberries are an especially welcome group of plants to those who roam the woodlands and fields late in the summer and on into the fall in search of their fruits. These gatherers include a great many species of wildlife as well as a large number of humans, and there is considerable competition for the sweet and spicy berries.

The erect and stiffly branching stems of this small deciduous shrub usually reach a height of no more than 2 or 3 feet. Many open areas are populated by blueberry colonies that are sometimes quite extensive.

The variable leaves are from 1 to 2 inches long and whitened beneath. They are usually oval and pointed with a narrowed base, though they may be wider and rounded at the tip.

The flowers that appear in May and June are greenish white to white and are generally flushed with pink or red. The petals are fused in the shape of a cylinder or urn or occasionally a sphere. Clusters of flowers are borne at the tips of the branches before the leaves have developed completely.

In June and July the green fruits begin to change to pink, then from July into September the clusters of immature pink and ripened dark blue berries are intermingled. These ripe berries are a quarter inch or more in diameter and whitened with a frostlike coating.

Somewhat similar are *V. angustifolium* and *V. stamineum,* but the former has smaller, narrower leaves, while the latter has more open flowers and larger acid fruits.

Low Blueberry, also called Dryland Blueberry and Late Low Blueberry, grows in dry open woods and clearings.

It does well on exposed slopes and rocky ground but must have an acid soil such as a mixture of sand and peat. It can be propagated by seeds or cuttings.

Low Blueberry

Vaccinium vacillans

Heath Family

Ericaceae

The slender brown stems are often armed with short sharp and thin spines at the base of the leaf stalks, and occasionally there are smaller prickles along the stem. Frequent and wide branching of the stems produces a dense, spreading shrub 2 to 4 feet tall. These shrubs, with their numerous thickly leaved stems, show up as rounded, dark green patches along mountain slopes and ridges.

The small leaves are usually nearly round in general outline. They are about 1 to 2 inches across and commonly have 3 lobes that are toothed along the margins.

The tiny flowers are green to reddish purple with protruding stamens. They occur singly or in small clusters of 2 or 3 during April and May.

The fruits develop slowly from June through September. These are round smooth berries nearly one-half inch in diameter that have a coloring of mottled purple. They are edible and are usually cooked in the preparation of jelly and pies.

There are 3 similar species, *R. americanum, R. cynosbati,* and *R. glandulosum,* in leaf and stem. The first has smooth black fruits; the remaining two have prickly fruits, but the last emits an unpleasant odor when bruised.

Wild Gooseberry has been given the names Smooth Gooseberry, Round-leaved Gooseberry, Mountain Wild Gooseberry, and Eastern Wild Gooseberry.

Mountain woods, clearings, and roadside banks are habitats of this species. It is an attractive small shrub that does well in almost any open area that has well drained soil, and it is especially well suited for rocky ground and slopes. It can be grown from seeds very easily. Cuttings and mound layering are also used as propagative measures.

Wild Gooseberry
Ribes rotundifolium

Saxifrage Family
Saxifragaceae

In late summer and autumn this perennial herb may have the appearance of a colorful tall shrub or small bushy tree. The large, deep green leaves flutter from the stout red-purple and widely branching stems at a height of 10 feet or more. The larger stems may be 1 to 2 inches in diameter, and the oblong, gradually tapering leaves are frequently a foot in length and half a foot wide.

Flowering begins in June and continues through the summer producing numerous long, tassellike clusters of small white flowers. The flowers are sometimes tinted with green or pink enhancing the attractiveness of the inflorescence; it is autumn, however, before this species reaches its pinnacle of beauty.

Through most of the summer the immature fruits develop progressively along the elongated flower clusters as flattened green berries. During September and October the most striking characteristics of the plant are all melded. The leaves retain their summer greenness, but the remainder of the tissues undergo a vivid transformation in color. All of the stems, leaf stalks, and fruit stalks are now a rich red-purple, and the berries exhibit a purple of high luster and of so dark a hue as to border on black.

Probably because of its uses as a food and a medicine and its poisonous properties, Pokeberry has accumulated several other names, among them, Poke, Skoke, Pokeweed, Garget, and Pigeonberry. Although young shoots have been cooked and used as greens and the fruit eaten by birds, the plant is dangerously poisonous, especially the roots and seeds.

This species is found in fields, roadsides, yards, pastures, and cultivated land. It is a highly ornamental plant, but is not recommended for grounds where children play.

Pokeberry

Phytolacca americana

Pokeweed Family

Phytolaccaceae

This straight-stemmed, interesting herb is about 2 or 3 feet tall and appears to have a multitude of lobed leaves clustered at the top. Actually the leafy apex of the plant consists of a single very large leaf that is divided and subdivided into many leaflets. There may be 1 or 2 much smaller leaves that originate from lower on the stem.

The flowering period comes during the months of April and May when the leaves are just beginning to expand. At the uppermost part of the stem there is a branching cluster of small, greenish yellow flowers that usually become tinged with maroon or purple.

The plant as a whole has a somewhat umbrellalike form that is attractive, and the intense green color and lobed shape of the many leaflets are further additions to its beauty. The flowers, which open while the leaves are still quite small, remain for some time as a centerpiece of unusual color that contrasts with the surrounding foliage. The most unusual and colorful feature of the plant, however, is revealed only after the fruiting process has gotten under way during July and August.

When the seeds begin to develop within the fruits, they grow at a faster rate than the tissues of the fruit wall. The pressure exerted on the wall by the enlarging seeds ruptures the developing fruit, whereupon it withers away. The only thing now visible is the seed which has the form of a sphere with a deep blue fleshy covering. This is usually mistaken for the fruit.

The leaves and seeds of Blue Cohosh contain a poisonous principle, and extracts from the underground parts were used by American Indians as a medicinal in connection with childbirth, which added the common name Papooseroot.

It grows in rich woods and is sometimes planted as an ornamental, but the toxic nature of the attractive "berries" may present a problem with children.

Blue Cohosh

Caulophyllum thalictroides

Barberry Family

Berberidaceae

A great many of the lowliest and most troublesome plants, those relegated to the netherworld of weeds, have their redeeming features. They may not be large, and they may be fleeting, but if one observes carefully and at the right time, some interesting and attractive combinations of pattern and pigmentation may be seen.

Field Garlic is such a one. The foliage is not impressive, and there is no colorful display of flowers or fruits. In many instances no flowers or fruits are produced at all. It has a widespread reputation as a highly undesirable species, yet there are a couple of times when some phases of its life cycle have a certain appeal.

The slender green stems grow from an underground bulb to a height sometimes exceeding 3 feet. The long leaves are slender tubes with much of their lower portion sheathing the stem. The entire plant has the odor of garlic.

Flowers develop from May to July at the tip of the stem in a small cluster that is at first enclosed within a pointed cover. The white, pink, or purple flowers are small but pretty with as many as 50 in a cluster, but again there may be few to none, their places taken by red-purple aerial bulbs.

When the clusters of flowers or bulbs enlarge, they break through the enclosing cover and carry it up with them. The bulbs usually have threadlike miniature leaves protruding from them, so that a bulb cluster somewhat resembles a hairy head wearing a papery, slender-beaked cap.

A similar species, *A. canadense,* has flat leaves, and the cover over the flowers and bulbs divides into 3 parts, producing no cap.

Field Garlic is also called Wild Onion and Crow Garlic. Cows eating either of these plants will pass the garlic flavor and odor on to the milk.

Both species are found in fields, roadsides, pastures, and lawns.

Field Garlic

Allium vineale

Wild Basil is a perennial herb prevalent in open areas of disturbed soils. Its simple or branching hairy stems are about 1 to 2 feet tall and frequently arise in small clumps from horizontal creeping rhizomes. Although not often mentioned in citations of prominent wildflowers, the deep rose-pink to red-purple flowers of late summer present a small but colorful picture. The arrangement of flowers forms a dense hemispherical to nearly spherical head which during the metamorphosis of fruiting changes from a green to a purplish or coppery brown many-pointed globe given a smoky effect by the presence of a multitude of fine white hairs.

The often square stems bear pairs of oval leaves having rounded or pointed tips and small-toothed to nearly smooth margins. They are about 1 to 2 inches long and almost stalkless toward the upper end of the stem.

Flower clusters appear at the stem tips and sometimes in the upper leaf axils from July to September. Flowers are about a half-inch long and usually pink or purple with white showing up infrequently.

The minute, dark brown, and rounded fruits develop within the 5-pointed tubular base of the flowers, and it is these floral structures that provide the form and color of the fruiting condition.

The culinary herb savory, *S. calamintha,* is an escape from cultivation that has no terminal flowers but has loosely few-flowered clusters in nearly all the leaf axils. *Blephilia ciliata* and *B. hirsuta* have 2 to several flower clusters in series around the upper stem; the former has lavender flowers, while the latter's are white. Wild Basil is referred to as Field Basil and Basil, but the basil of commerce is of the genus *Ocimum*. Other herbs of cookery in the genus *Satureja* are Basil-thyme, *S. calamintha,* and Mother-of-thyme, *S. acinos.*

Wild Basil grows in open woods, thickets, fields, roadsides, and pastures.

Wild Basil

Satureja vulgaris

Many of the branches of this highly floriferous little tree become wrapped in a rose pink to reddish purple blanket during April and May when the flowers open. The flowers are about one-half-inch long and resemble pea or bean flowers. They are produced in small clusters of 2 to 8 flowers, and those stems formed in the previous year, and occasionally the trunk, are densely populated with these clusters.

The flowers are ordinarily fully open before any leaves appear. They are broadly heart-shaped and generally as wide as or wider than they are long. The form and dark green color of these leaves make for a handsome foliage.

The slender trunk sends out stems fairly close to the ground that grow in a spreading and irregular branching pattern. The result is a relatively short tree with a broad crown that is often unusual in form but almost always attractive in its asymmetry.

Redbud has long been a favorite as one of those plants that show an early abundance of bright color after the winter. The pink and purple of the flowers along with the verdant foliage are cited often for their color contribution to spring and summer, but the fruits are commonly overlooked in this respect.

The fruit is a flattened pod that tapers to a point at both ends. At first green, the color changes to tan, rust, purplish brown, or bronze. They usually hang from the tree in thick clusters from June to November and add a beauty of a different kind to summer and fall.

Judas Iscariot is said to have hanged himself from a redbud, so the name Judas Tree is also used for this tree.

Redbud is found in moist woods frequently on fairly steep slopes. It is a popular plant for ornamental planting and can be grown from seed.

Redbud

Cercis canadensis

Pulse Family

Leguminosae

A spreading shrub 3 to 10 feet tall, this species provides the wetlands with several colors through the seasons. The dark green foliage of spring and summer shows flashes of red-purple from the young branches. About midsummer there is a scattering of white flower clusters followed by the blue fruits of autumn.

Stems vary in color from green to greenish brown and purple and bear fine silky hairs. Lower branches often bend downward in contact with the soil.

The leaves grow in pairs and are 2 to 4 inches long. The blade is oval and tapered abruptly to a point toward which all the veins curve.

The very small flowers are white to pale yellow, their 4 petals forming a diminutive cross. They are in flattened, dome-shaped clusters two or three inches across. Flowering takes place in May and June.

Rounded and somewhat flattened blue berrylike fruits ripen in September and October. Their color varies from a pale blue to a dusky grayish blue, and occasionally white ones are seen.

Dogwoods have similar flowers and paired leaves, but *C. alternifolia* has unpaired leaves. *C. racemosa* has pyramidal flower and fruit clusters and white fruits. The familiar Flowering Dogwood, *C. florida,* has flower clusters that appear to be a large flower, and *C. canadensis,* a small herb, has a single "flower" of that kind.

Silky Dogwood is known also as Silky Cornel, Swamp Dogwood, Red Willow, and Kinnikinnik, which refers to a bark and tobacco mixture smoked by the American Indians.

This plant grows in swamps, marshes, and wet woods. It is a valuable species for providing cover and food for wildlife species, in addition to which it is a hardy and handsome shrub that can be grown from seed that germinate the second year.

Silky Dogwood

Cornus amomum

Dogwood Family

Cornaceae

Light green red-stalked leaves are clustered near the tips of spaced whorls of branches that radiate horizontally from the main stem to produce a layered, pagodalike effect. A host of broad, rounded flower clusters open at the tips of the branches in late spring and early summer spangling the tiers of foliage with splashes of white. The ripening of fruits that comes in late summer and autumn creates an additional hue, and the white spangles become bicolored as the shiny blue-black berrylike fruits mature on purplish red stalks. And the seasonal alterations of environmental factors eventually replace the green of the foliage with scarlet.

Pagoda Dogwood develops as a shrub 4 to 15 feet tall or as a tree in excess of 20 feet high. The stems are greenish brown to purplish red.

The oval leaves are tapered at both ends and differ from other dogwoods in that they are not paired but are alternately arranged on the stems.

The flowers of May and June are small and are produced in open clusters that are flat-topped to hemispherical.

The fruits are slightly flattened spheres a little less than half an inch in diameter that are red when immature and ripen dark blue to deep blue-black.

Other dogwoods are similar in foliage and flower, but fruits of *C. amomum* are light blue. Flower clusters of *C. florida* appear as a single large flower. Fruits of *C. racemosa* are white, and the leaves of *C. rugosa* are nearly round.

Pagoda Dogwood, also named Alternate-leaved Dogwood, Blue Dogwood, and Green Osier, finds a home in rich woods, shrub balds, low roadsides, and stream banks.

This is a highly desirable ornamental for sunny or shady sites, offering an interesting branching pattern, floral and fruiting showiness, and vivid fall color. Seeds will germinate the second year after planting.

Pagoda Dogwood

Cornus alternifolia

Dogwood Family

Cornaceae

In the early summer a rash of large, yellowish green and spherical flower clusters stand up from a sizable bank of bright green foliage on very long, straight stalks that turn magenta in the fall and bend under the weight of the blue-black fruits. A twisting maze rises, not infrequently to a height of 10 feet, from the tangled growth of this herbaceous vine as the long, smooth stems branch freely and climb by threadlike tendrils over other plants and themselves.

The ovate to almost round leaves are 2 to 5 inches long and are often whitened on the under surfaces.

The small flowers are either male or female on separate plants, so that some plants show no fruits. The opening blossoms in May and June are accompanied by an odor said by many to approximate that of decaying meat, whence came the name.

The fruits mature from August to October as dark blue to black berries that are tightly packed in globular clusters hanging from the long, drooping stalks.

The species *S. ecirrhata* is a more erect plant without tendrils. There are 3 species with prickly woody stems. *S. glauca* has leaves much whitened beneath, *S. rotundifolia* has flowering stalks about the length of the leaf stalks, and *S. hispida* has much longer flowering stalks and dark flexible prickles.

Many woody species of the genus *Smilax,* called Catbrier or Greenbrier, have been used as a source of medicinals. Bark extracts were used to make tonics and toothache painkillers, and it is especially interesting to note that root and stem preparations were employed both as an aphrodisiac and in treatment of venereal disease. It is not known which came first.

Carrion Flower is found in moist woods and thickets, coves, meadows, and low roadsides. It is not a species recommended for planting, although there are some who say that the floral odor really isn't that bad.

Carrion Flower

Smilax herbacea

The leafy stems of Solomon's Seal curve gracefully from the vegetational fabric that carpets the moist woodland floors throughout the region. In the spring from the bases of the leaves emerge the pendulous flowers that hang on the undersides of these arching stems like clusters of slender miniature bells of white, green, or yellow. When autumn comes, the place of the bells is taken by the black or dark-blue berries.

The stems vary from slender to stout and arise from a rhizome, or subterranean stem. The height of the plant varies from nearly a foot to more than 6 feet. Often the stems and leaves have a whitish to bluish coating that rubs off. The upper portion of the stem bears many broad, stalkless leaves that are pointed and 2 to 8 inches long.

The flowers of May and June may occur singly but are usually produced in clusters of 2 to 9. They are tubular with flared tips and colored white to pale yellow with varied tinting of green.

The fruits ripen from August to October as berries that are about a half-inch in diameter and spherical. The color ranges from blue to blue-black or black. Eating of the berries is reported to cause nausea.

Another species, *P. pubescens,* is more erect with less stem curvature, and the undersurfaces of the leaves are hairy.

The name Common Solomon's Seal is used when the species is split into two. The larger plants are then designated *P. canaliculatum* with the common name Great Solomon's Seal.

These plants are common to moist wooded areas. They are frequently planted in wildflower gardens and fare well in either partially shaded or completely shaded situations. The soil should be deep and rich to prevent drying.

Propagation is best effected by division of the underground stems.

Solomon's Seal

Polygonatum biflorum

This shrub or small tree comonly 4 to 10 feet tall occasionally ranges upward to about 30 feet. The fairly stout and softly hairy stems are gray-brown or sometimes reddish and bear large glossy and many-parted leaves. Broad pyramidal clusters of green to greenish yellow flowers are conspicuous at the tops of the branches in summer, and when autumn arrives these pymamids nod with the weight of the dense masses of small lavender to crimson fruits. The vivid hues of fruiting are matched by the changing of the foliage.

Many of the leaves are a foot in length, with their blades composed of several to many oblong pointed leaflets. There are narrow, winglike projections from the central stalk of the leaf between the leaflets.

Flowers open in July and August in clusters as much as a foot long. The flowers are very small and are produced in great quantity.

The berrylike fruits are tiny and covered with short hairs. As they mature they pass through several shades of red and purple and finally ripen crimson.

There are three somewhat similar species. Both *R. typhina* and *R. glabra* have toothed leaflets, but the latter has smooth stems. Fortunately *R. vernix* is rare in the mountains. It is powerfully poisonous. It is a small tree of swamps and wet ground 6 to 20 feet tall, having leaves with smooth-margined toothless leaflets and fruits that are white.

Winged Sumac has been given the additional names of Shining Sumac, Dwarf Sumac, Mountain Sumac, and Black Sumac. Due to the high content of tannins in its leaves and bark, it has been put to use in the tanning of leather.

This is a plant of dry woods, fields, roadsides, rocky slopes; thus it is an excellent choice for planting in exposed sunny areas with dry soils and is ornamental through the year. It can be grown from seeds planted in the fall or from root cuttings.

Winged Sumac

Rhus copallina

Cashew Family

Anacardiaceae

Moist and rich wooded slopes in the mountains are liberally dotted during the spring of the year with the tufts of dark green and shining leaves overtopped by clusters of small speckled white flowers. When the flowering is done and the withered remnants have fallen to the ground, the autumn season sees a second display of beauty different in form and color. The durable leaves retain their attractiveness and are now spread beneath clusters of berries of a black or deep blue hue.

The plants appear to be stemless, since the leaves and flowering stalks arise from a rootstock, or underground stem. The clumps of 2 to 5 glossy leaves that seemingly sprout directly from the soil are 6 to 12 inches long and as much as 4 inches wide.

The flowers of May and June are small, but they develop in conspicuous clusters at the tip of a slender leafless stalk 8 to 12 inches long. The petals are greenish white to white with purple tips and a sprinkling of purple specks.

The flowers are succeeded during August to October by berries that are small, about a third of an inch in diameter, but like the flowers are highly visible as a group. The color of these fruits varies from a dark blue to black.

There is another species, *C. borealis,* that has leaves extremely similar to Speckled Wood Lily, and the general form of the plant is the same. The berries of the former are light bright blue, and the flowers are larger and yellow.

Speckled Wood Lily is also known as White Clintonia. The generic name commemorates DeWitt Clinton, a naturalist and strong advocate of the Erie Canal, known at first as "Clinton's Ditch."

This species is found in rich mountain woods. It can be grown from seeds or from planting the underground stems in a cool moist site.

Speckled Wood Lily

Clintonia umbellulata

Lily Family

Liliaceae

Black Haw may develop as a large shrub or small tree. Its stout stems are often crooked and are thickly branched to form a spreading crown. Its height ranges from 4 or 5 feet to about 15 feet.

The paired leaves are short-stalked and oval with finely toothed margins. Blades are usually 1 to 3 inches long and wider near the middle. The tips are mostly pointed but can be rounded and wider than the base.

Flowering comes in April and May when the leaves are not yet fully developed. The small white flowers form many large and dense flat-topped clusters.

The fragrant flowers in their many showy clusters make a fine spring display against their leafy green background, but autumn brings an even more colorful time for Black Haw. During September and October the summer green of the foliage becomes a purplish red, as the fruits proceed through their color alterations from green through orange and red to blue or black. The ripe fruit is oval and berrylike about a half-inch long. The color is usually black or dark blue-black, and occasionally there is a touch of frosty coating. In addition to their beauty they serve as food for many wildlife species.

The leaves of *V. alnifolium* and *V. acerifolium* are much larger; those of the former are nearly round, while the latter's are lobed and toothed. The leaves of *V. rafinesquianum* and *V. dentatum* have larger teeth, and the former's are more pointed, narrow, and nearly stalkless, while the latter has wider and more rounded leaves. The leaves of *V. cassinoides* and *V. nudum* have small reddish brown spots underneath; otherwise the two species are very similar.

Black Haw, also called Sweet Haw, Nanny Berry, and Stagbush, is recommended by its early floral showiness, its early green and late red foliage, and unusually colorful fruiting procession. Its habitats are moist and dry woods, and it can be grown from seeds or cuttings in almost any kind of soil.

Black Haw

Viburnum prunifolium

Honeysuckle Family

Caprifoliaceae

The long stems of this grapevine generally possess loose bark that frequently splits and peels away in strips. Older stems may grow to be several inches thick trailing over low vegetation, but they also are often observed high among the limbs of some of the tallest trees. From the side of the stem opposite a great many of the leaf stalks there extends a slender curling tendril by means of which the vine climbs. Opposite nearly all of the other leaf stalks there is a flowering or fruiting cluster. Young branches may possess small tufts of soft hairs.

The leaves are large and broadly heart-shaped to nearly round. Their blades are toothed and sometimes shallowly lobed with a length and width of 3 to 8 inches. The upper surface is dull green and smooth, while the underside is covered with a dense growth of reddish brown or gray hairs.

The time of flowering comes in May and June, and great numbers of tiny but fragrant yellowish to greenish blossoms are produced. They are arranged in elongate and pendulous clusters from 1 to 3 inches long.

The grapes mature in August and September in rather short compact clusters of usually not more than 20. Their color is reddish brown to purplish black, sometimes with a light whitish coating or bloom when ripe. They are larger than most other wild grapes at one-half to three-quarters of an inch or more.

A similar species is *V. aestivalis,* but many leaves lack an accompanying tendril or flowering or fruiting cluster. The grapes are smaller, and the leaves are usually much more deeply lobed.

Fox Grape, also called Northern Fox Grape and Skunk Grape, is the parent of several varieties of cultivated grapes including Concord. Grapes are good choices for practical and ornamental planting and are easily grown from seeds.

Fox Grape

Vitis labrusca

Vine Family

Vitaceae

Pronunciation Key to Scientific Names

The symbols ` and ´ mark the syllable to be accented; the former calls for a long vowel sound, while the latter calls for a short vowel sound.

Anacardiàceae
  Rhùs aromática
  Rhùs copallìna
  Rhùs glàbra
  Rhùs radìcans
Annonàceae
  Asímina tríloba
Aquifoliàceae
  Ìlex verticillàta
Aràceae
  Arisaèma triphýllum
Araliàceae
  Aràlia nudicaùlis
  Pànax quinquefòlius
Asclepiadàceae
  Asclèpias syrìaca
Balsaminàceae
  Impàtiens capénsis
Berberidàceae
  Berbèris thunbèrgii
  Caulophýllum thalictroìdes
  Jeffersònia diphýlla
Bignoniàceae
  Catálpa specìòsa
Caprifoliàceae
  Lonícera mórrowi
  Sambùcus pùbens
  Vibúrnum prunifòlium
Celastràceae
  Celástrus scándens
  Euónymus americànus
Compósitae
  Bìdens bipinnàta
  Círsium vulgàre
  Tragopògon májor
  Xánthium strumàrium
Cornàceae
  Córnus a·nòmum
  ... a·ˈernifòlia
  Córnus flórida

Córnus flórida
Corylàceae
  Álnus serrulàta
  Bétula lénta
  Córylus cornùta
  Óstrya virginiàna
Crucíferae
  Lepídium campéstre
  Lunària ánnua
  Nastúrtium officinàle
  Thláspi arvénse
Dioscoreàceae
  Dioscorèa villòsa
Dipsacàceae
  Dípsacus sylvéstris
Elaeagnàceae
  Elaeágnus umbellàta
Equisetàceae
  Equisètum hyemàle
Ericàceae
  Kálmia latifòlia
  Rhododéndron catawbiénse
  Vaccìnium macrocárpon
  Vaccìnium vacíllans
Fagàceae
  Castànea pùmila
Geraniàceae
  Gerànium caroliniànum
Gramíneae
  Setària fabèrii
  Unìola latifòlia
Hamamelidàceae
  Hamamèlis virginiàna
Juglandàceae
  Jùglans cinèrea
Labiàtae
  Saturèja vulgàris
Lauràceae
  Líndera benzòin
  Sássafras álbidum

203

Leguminòsae
  Cércis canadénsis
  Desmòdium nudiflòrum
  Gledítsia triacánthos
  Robínia pseùdo-acàcia
Liliàceae
  Állium vineàle
  Aspáragus offícinalis
  Clintònia umbellulàta
  Maiánthemum canadénse
  Medèola virginiàna
  Polygónatum biflòrum
  Smilacìna racemòsa
  Smìlax herbàcea
Loranthàceae
  Phoradéndron flavéscens
Magnoliàceae
  Magnòlia acuminàta
Malvàceae
  Abùtilon theophrásti
Moràceae
  Mòrus álba
Oleàceae
  Ligústrum sinénse
Osmundàceae
  Osmúnda regàlis
Oxalidàceae
  Óxalis europaèa
Papaveràceae
  Papàver dùbium
Passifloràceae
  Passiflòra incarnàta
Phytolaccàceae
  Phytolácca americàna
Ranunculàceae
  Actaèa pachýpoda
  Aquilègia canadénsis

Clématis virginiàna
Hydrástis canadénsis
Rosàceae
  Amelánchier arbòrea
  Crataègus uniflòra
  Duchésnea índica
  Physocárpus opulifòlius
  Prùnus seròtina
  Pýrus americàna
  Rìbes rotundifòlium
  Ròsa carolìna
  Rùbus odoràtus
  Rùbus phoenicolàsius
Rubiàceae
  Cephalánthus occidentàlis
  Gàlium aparìne
  Mitchélla rèpens
Salicàceae
  Sàlix rígida
Saxifragàceae
  Rìbes rotundifòlium
Scrophulariàceae
  Paulównia tomentòsa
Simaroubàceae
  Ailánthus altíssima
Solanàceae
  Datùra stramònium
  Solànum dulcamàra
Staphyleàceae
  Staphylèa trifòlia
Typhàceae
  Týpha latifòlia
Umbellíferae
  Osmorhìza longistýlis
Vitàceae
  Vìtis labrúsca

Index of Common and Scientific Names

Boldface page numbers refer to illustrations.